HIGH-IMPACT TRAINING SOLUTIONS

TOP ISSUES TROUBLING TRAINERS

Edited by Lisa A. Burke

Foreword by Dana Gaines Robinson

QUORUM BOOKS
Westport, Connecticut • London

Library of Congress Cataloging-in-Publication Data

High-impact training solutions : top issues troubling trainers / edited by Lisa A. Burke ; foreword by Dana Gaines Robinson.
    p.   cm.
   Includes bibliographical references and index.
   ISBN 1–56720–446–5 (alk. paper)
   1. Employees—Training of.   2. Strategic planning.   I. Burke, Lisa A., 1966–
HF5549.5.T7H535   2001
   658.3′124—dc21   2001018026

British Library Cataloguing in Publication Data is available.

Library of Congress Catalog Card Number: 2001018026
ISBN: 1–56720–446–5

First published in 2001

Quorum Books, 88 Post Road West, Westport, CT 06881
An imprint of Greenwood Publishing Group, Inc.
www.quorumbooks.com

Printed in the United States of America

The paper used in this book complies with the Permanent Paper Standard issued by the National Information Standards Organization (Z39.48–1984).

10 9 8 7 6 5 4 3 2 1

Copyright Acknowledgments

Chapter 2 (usage of client name and actual case history): E-mail permission granted, from Charles Farkas, dated 8/2/00. Used with permission.

Chapter 6 (reprint of an ISPI figure): E-mail permission granted, from Matthew Davis, ISPI, 10/30/00. Used with permission.

Chapter 7 quote: Quote from THE WAY OF THE SHAMAN by MICHAEL HARNER. Copyright © 1980 by Michael Harner. Reprinted by permission of HarperCollins Publishers, Inc.

To CHRIS AND OUR FAMILIES

CONTENTS

ILLUSTRATIONS

TABLES

FIGURES

FOREWORD

PERFORMANCE ... a word we hear with frequency in today's highly competitive, challenging business environment—performance of the business, performance of equipment, performance of information and high-tech systems. In the Training/Human Resource Development (HRD) professions, we are also focused on performance—performance of people. For too long, our primary professional focus has been on the solutions used to impact human performance, as though these solutions were "the end result" provided. Did people enjoy the training experience? Did they learn in it? Was the case study a good one? And now, added to this mix, are questions regarding whether the learning experience should be electronically mediated rather than leader-led. All of these are critical issues to consider. But, in the end, the real issue is whether people's performance on-the-job has been enhanced. Solutions are *not* the end—they are a means to the end.

This brings us to the present book. A few years ago, research was conducted on attendees at major training conferences in North America. These individuals were asked to identify issues that were most troubling them. The results? Trainers indicated several issues were challenging them. Some were very tactical in nature, such as how to identify *true* training needs and how to integrate e-learning options in an effective manner. Some were strategic in nature—for example, how to enhance skill transfer from training programs and how to become more linked to the "business-of-the-business." What all the issues had in common was a need to ensure that learning solutions *do* enhance human performance and positively contribute to business results.

It is these questions and issues, on the minds of trainers, which form the basis for this book. What I find exciting about this book is that it is a practical guide to best practices relative to challenges shared in common by training professionals across multiple industries. These issues are not faddish; rather, they have continued to challenge those of us in the profession for years. The authors of chapters in this book are practitioners—some in an external consultant role and some working internal to one organization. Each author has personally experienced the challenges discussed and provides best practices and techniques that can be used immediately. These are not arcane, theoretical discussions—they are written from the "been there, done that" perspective.

This book is not intended to be an "all there is to know" about any of the issues discussed. Rather, it provides you with in-depth, practical insights for beginning or continuing your journey of learning, relative to the topics covered. If you are advanced in your journey in one area (such as embracing a new role like performance consultant), you can read a specific chapter for affirmation of what you are doing. For issues that you are only beginning to address (perhaps e-learning and technology-based approaches to learning), you can view the relevant chapter to learn about how to begin and what to consider in starting. In other words, each chapter has nuggets to glean regardless of where you are personally. And if you want to learn more, each chapter has a list of references to guide you as you investigate the topic further. In addition, a suggested resources section is located at the end.

Enhancing human performance *must* be the result of our collective work as trainers. I trust that the wisdom provided by the authors in this book will assist you in this goal. In so doing, you will be making performance *your* business.

Dana Gaines Robinson
Coauthor, *Performance Consulting*
Pittsburgh, Pennsylvania

Preface

The objective of this book is to directly address the most pressing issues in the training and development field. The specific issues that are addressed include the following: the strategic linkage of training to organizational goals, the determination of training vs. nontraining needs, training technologies, the transfer of training to the job, the growing emphasis on a holistic performance perspective, and lastly, the multiple, yet expanding, number of hats trainers are wearing in organizations. Some of these issues hit at the core of a trainer's traditional responsibilities, such as needs assessment, while others have appeared more recently on the trainer's horizon as an enduring challenge to tackle (for example, strategically linking training to business objectives, new training technologies, holistic training and development).

The various contributing authors, all of whom have extensive professional, consulting, and/or research experience in the training field, thoroughly examine these leading training issues. Yet they do so, not from an abstract, convoluted perspective, but by speaking directly and straightforwardly to the training professional—whether internal or external to an organization—and attempting to address their needs. For example, the book provides the training practitioner (or any reader who has an interest in, affiliation with, or desire to learn about training) with relevant frameworks, revealing examples and real-life cases and specific recommendations. Please note that the identities of organizations and individuals involved in any case examples based to some degree on real-life cases are not revealed; fictitious names are used (unless otherwise noted).

Each author tells a relevant story and provides direction to the reader, yet allows for the professional's individual style and consideration of his or her organizational context. This is expressly because there is not one exact or specific way to execute the various steps in the training process across all organizations and situations. Furthermore, references are provided throughout each chapter to support key findings that are presented, to note the most prominent training research, and to provide the reader with a comprehensive resource base. In sum, this book offers many clear specifications about the training issues at hand—what we know, what we have experienced, and how we can creatively manage these most-talked-about training issues.

What may be more telling to the reader, however, is a description about what this book is not. It is not a comprehensive "tools" book, a basic training and development primer, an overview of the entire training process, a faddish look at the training function, or a detached, convoluted text. We do not try to dazzle readers with faddish buzzwords, trendy applications, or scientific jargon that few can understand. Instead, our goal is to reach out to front-line training professionals straightforwardly, so that they can achieve high impact in their training endeavors. Clearly, it is in the hands of these individuals that the training departments throughout the world will continue to move forward, with a heightened level of sophistication. Our job, as authors then, is to guide practitioners in their various roles and help them to generate high-impact training.

The book's genesis comes in part from reviewing a summary of data collected from training practitioners at recent training and development conferences (for example, American Society for Training and Development and Training '99 Conference and Expo) regarding the issues in their jobs troubling them most (refer to: http://www.growthworksinc.com/trouble.pdf). Using this as the primary source of topics for the book, we have reached out and listened to those on the forefront of training and are explicitly responding to their concerns.

To all those individuals who have anything (and everything) to do with organizational training and development, my hat goes off to you. This is a challenging area to work in; I know because of having been there and continuing to interact with many training professionals from diverse firms who face myriad challenges. Not unlike most of our organizational counterparts, many trainers are trying to do more with less, juggle many projects simultaneously, wear various hats, meet numerous deadlines, and so on. At the same time, let us be reminded that training is an extremely rewarding area to work in given its direct and indirect impact on the firm's most bona fide asset—people.

For those who look to stay in the training and development field (as an internal trainer or external consultant), due to its mission and personal interests, you have an important and expanding role in guiding others through the many changes in today's organizations. You will experience burgeoning visibility to the extent that you engage in high-impact training practices, and this visibility will in turn translate into credibility and influence. The profession needs you to succeed and help transform others' thinking regarding this field.

For those internal training practitioners who aspire to positions in other functional areas of their organization, the training department is a good area to develop and reveal your potential. There is a growing amount of high-level management exposure in training departments, involvement in critical business decisions, and access to all parts of the firm's managers and employees. Your tasks include expanding your training expertise, making a clear impact, and then continuing to carry the training torch while navigating through different areas in the organization. In other words, you will be important champions of training internally.

Management training, development, and education are my absolute professional passion. Nothing warms my heart more than exciting others about my discipline—seeing the eyes of a truly engaged learner, giving career advice to students, soliciting and supporting learner involvement, and sitting back and watching others grow and develop over time, beyond my expectations. In that way, I'm fortunate to be so enthusiastic about my professional endeavors. Not surprisingly then, I look forward to sharing my passion about training and development with readers by way of this book.

Such an edited book would not be possible without help from a number of people. I want to thank Hilary Claggett and the Quorum staff, as well as Ken Coar for assistance early on in the project. I also very much appreciate the time invested by those who read earlier versions of this work and provided comments and feedback, including Dana Robinson, Kevin Ford, and Scott Parry. As busy as they are, they agreed to share their effort and energy with me. Thanks also to Lisa Cheraskin and Tim Baldwin for their cultivation of my early interest in this field. Most importantly, special thanks go to the terrific group of contributors who embraced this authorship challenge whole-heartedly and delivered a high-quality product. It was my pleasure to work with them and to learn from them as well.

Finally, I want to thank Ruby and my husband, Chris, along with our families, for being so supportive throughout the writing process. Their genuine interest and concern in this project added fuel to my fire and undoubtedly facilitated my ability to efficiently produce a better end product.

Chapter 1

INTRODUCTION

Lisa A. Burke

What an exciting time to be involved with employee learning, training, and development in organizations. With the growing talk of "learning organizations," "knowledge management," "chief learning officers" and so on, the training and development area is finally starting to get its deserved time in the organizational spotlight. All of us who are involved in training—either as consultants, trainers, researchers, managers, professors, students, analysts, strategists, and so on—have witnessed an increasing level of sophistication of the modern day training professional, and a growing appreciation for that expertise. It is therefore exhilarating to see the discipline flowering and finally coming into its own.

For too long, many organizational leaders thought that there was no "science" to training and development. The training function was all too often used as a dumping ground for employees who could not cut it elsewhere in the firm, and training departments had to fight for every dime in their budget. No wonder, the training and development function's credibility and effectiveness took a direct hit—how can effective training interventions even be generated in this type of environment? Granted, there is an art to certain training activities such as gaining and holding the interest of an audience or designing that one special exercise that seems to drive the learning point home. But there is also accumulating a body of knowledge and well-founded experience (that is., "the science of training"), which can work to enhance training outcomes in the new business reality.

This level of refinement to the training discipline does not come without additional responsibilities, however. With our increasingly expert role in organizations come accountability and expectations for bottom-line business results for what we do. Cutting-edge firms, such as Motorola, General Electric, and Sun Microsystems, place training or learning responsibilities at the forefront in their organization. Clearly, top managers respect the value that training adds to their firm's competitive spirit, yet each of these firms and their top managers undoubtedly expect a return on their training investment in some form. Thus, we must be cognizant, as trainers, of our duty, role, and responsibility.

It is clear that those on the leading cusp of training practices understand and appreciate the role that training plays within the larger human resource and organizational context. Neglecting this system perspective produces myopic, deficient, and short-term training responses and interventions that can keep the training function in the proverbial back seat. In the next section, the importance of viewing training and development as a subsystem of human resources (HR) is addressed.

TRAINING AS A SUBSYSTEM OF HUMAN RESOURCES

Perhaps one of the biggest pitfalls that any training or human resource practitioner can fall into is forgetting the bigger picture, or contextual basis, in which the subsystems of HR coexist. The training professional who not only appreciates this system perspective but actively calls upon it and applies it to everyday training challenges will add the most value to his organization. Admittedly, this is a hard reality to achieve, especially when individuals have tried to hone their command of a certain HR area; however, training personnel should strive to simultaneously embody a deepened expertise and ability to stand back and see how HR subsystems impact each other. Let's analyze this a bit further by discussing HR as a system and the role of training and development as depicted in figure 1.1.

As illustrated in figure 1.1, HR planning, recruiting, selection, compensation, performance appraisal, and training and development compose the human resource system. These subsystems all are interrelated as well. For example, the quality of a firm's recruiting and staffing functions will directly impact the organization's need for training. Should new employees' skills not quite meet company needs, for example, the training and development function will need to bolster them. And performance appraisal results directly drive the need for training, as organizations typically attempt (or should attempt) to remedy their current employees' skill deficits. Just as training can directly enhance employee performance, so too can beefing up recruiting and selection standards, developing effectual performance appraisal and coaching systems, and offering compensation packages that motivate employees.

Figure 1.1
Training as a Subsystem of Human Resources

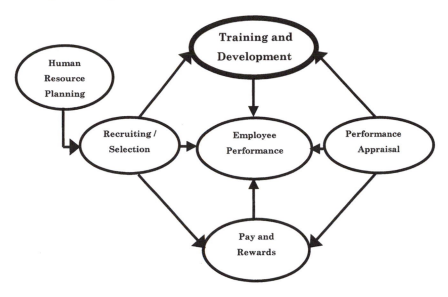

Human resource practitioners need to acknowledge and act upon these subsystem interactions in order to create effective HR solutions. Consider the following hypothetical, yet realistic, scenario. If a manufacturing plant faces the reality of dramatically converting its assembly line processes to a computer-integrated manufacturing (CIM) system with self-directed work teams, it has numerous HR decisions to make. Should it hire new employees who have the knowledge and skills to work in this drastically different environment or take the preexisting employee base (or some portion of it) and train them to work in the new CIM environment, or some combination thereof? How should team performance be managed, appraised, and facilitated and how should the compensation scheme change to accommodate a team-driven approach? These are just some of the questions that need to be asked. Those of us who specialize in a given HR niche, such as training, need to stand back in these situations and see the bigger picture of how other HR solutions may be preferred, necessary, or beneficial.

TRAINING AS A SYSTEMATIC PROCESS

Not only is training part of a larger system, but training in and of itself is also a systematic process. All subparts, or phases, of the training system are directly or indirectly interrelated. In figure 1.2, a representation of the basic elements of a systematic approach to training is outlined.

Specifically, the first step in the training process is to conduct a needs assessment to determine if a training intervention is needed (and if so, who

Figure 1.2
Training as a System

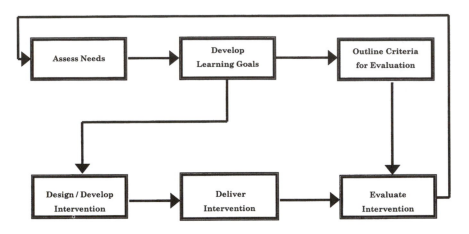

needs it and what do they need). From the needs assessment, specific learning or training objectives are articulated, which help to determine the criteria against which the intervention will ultimately be evaluated. Learning objectives also drive the design, development, and delivery of the intervention. And finally, an evaluation can measure trainees' reactions to the program, their learning, and their behavioral change on the job. All of these subparts are ultimately interdependent. For example, needs assessment forms the foundation upon which everything else is built, and evaluation results can encourage the revision of the entire training process, or certain phases within it.

The issues that we straightforwardly tackle in this book, in explicit and direct response to trainers' recently voiced concerns, are most closely related to needs assessment and the design and delivery of training. Training evaluation is also addressed, especially in the holistic training and transfer of training chapters, although to a lesser extent than other core training areas.

Ultimately, embracing a systems perspective is only one of the marks of a mature training function. Additional elements are addressed in the next section, which also indicate a high-impact approach to training and development (Noe, 1999).

INDICATORS OF HIGH-IMPACT TRAINING

Today, more training staffs and departments are adding value in organizations by embracing a high-impact approach. First, high-impact trainers are players in, or at least privy to, top management decisions in their organization. Trainers can no longer afford to be the "last-to-know" or "first-to-go" in relation to major business decisions and changes. As an example, many mergers, acquisitions, divestitures, reorganizations, and other structural changes in firms have created havoc for many employees as they take on new, broader, and/or different roles, jobs, and tasks. In these situations, employees may need support in the form of on-the-job and/or formal training. By being at the head table during these organizational changes, training professionals can identify and address the learning and training implications associated with impending structural change.

High-impact training departments also aim to support changes in business strategy. If, for example, an organization is pursuing a cost leadership business strategy, then the content of management development programs should support this theme and focus. Otherwise there will be a serious disconnect between training and the larger business context. Or if customer service must be the firm's primary thrust in order to gain competitive advantage in its industry, then training should be linked to this specific business focus.

This point was evident in a recent discussion with the general manager of a cleaners and laundry business. First of all, he does not consider himself to be in the cleaners business. Rather, he says, he is in the customer service business and wants all his employees to understand that fact. In order to achieve and maintain superior customer service, this general manager said it was imperative to hire a full-time trainer to work with and improve the performance of his front-line employees. The most important fact is not that he hired a trainer, but that he said the trainer had "paid for herself" (that is, her direct salary) in a matter of about five months due to fewer employee mistakes made throughout business processes as a result of her training efforts. As this example reveals, if training supports a business's strategy, it will add value and it will create high impact.

To achieve this impact, we are seeing organizations enlisting the aid of more experts in training subfields and subdisciplines. As such, there is a likely evolution that occurs in the development of many training departments. Typically, training departments start out small, with small budgets, and are staffed by internally rotated employees who become training generalists. But once the training staff's value is demonstrated, especially in larger organizations, managers (and the transplanted trainer) will likely realize that more training expertise is needed in order for comprehensive training impact to occur.

Perhaps the organization requires expertise in the training subprocesses of needs assessment, program design and development, training transfer, and/or program evaluation. Granted, the firm can either meet this need by staffing full-time employees (who are hired as experts in their training discipline), or by contracting with external consultants who are experts in a given area, whichever is more economically feasible and effective long-term. Regardless, the need for a sophisticated training approach is increasingly being identified, sought out, and integrated into organizations in order to formulate a more mature training presence that meets organizational needs to improve performance.

In these situations, high-impact trainers have evolved broadly into performance consultants or human performance technologists—examining the various causes of lackluster employee performance via performance gap analysis (see, for example, Wile, 1996) and determining the most appropriate solution, whatever it may be. High-impact training departments are able to get beyond complying with the all-too-common management request of "we need a training program on X." Instead, they understand the power of needs assessment, and by employing their expertise in assessing performance discrepancies, they are better equipped to communicate with managers why training may, or may not (!), be the best solution. And when a training intervention is needed, they are able to achieve on-the-job performance improvements by ensuring that employees transfer or use their newly attained knowledge, skills, and abilities back on the job.

High-impact training staffs succeed, in large measure, by building trusting relationships with line managers. Granted, without upper management support, hardly any area in a firm can be successful. But securing this positive, supportive relationship is the sine qua non of high-impact training departments. Achieving this type of relationship may be difficult (and seen unattainable to some of us), but undoubtedly critical. It may sound like a cliché, but trainers must get managers involved; they cannot achieve real, lasting results without them. The sooner all trainers realize and embrace this fact, the further ahead in the marathon they will be.

Now, this view may sound too idealistic. But it is important to note that this is the reality that leading-edge firms and their training personnel have created! High-impact training practices have been documented and are not impossible to achieve. It has been the Steve Kerrs (of General Electric) and the Ken Hansens (of Xerox) who have set the precedent. But it also takes the commitment and involvement of everyone—from the CEO to the line manager to the new training associate—to make it a reality. We hope in this book to aid training professionals in striving for high-impact training practices. As such, the next section provides an overview of each chapter which addresses an issue of paramount concern to trainers who are aiming for high-impact status.

OVERVIEW OF THE BOOK CHAPTERS

The objective of this book is to directly address the most pressing issues troubling trainers, so that they can better design, develop, and deliver interventions that improve employee performance and create competitive advantage. These chapters are in direct response to trainers' voiced concerns, as noted in the preface, and tap issues at the very core of traditional trainer responsibilities, as well as new challenges that lie on the trainer's horizon.

The first contributor in this book addresses strategic training, or the use of training and development as a business solution. Joseph Wilson III, corporate veteran, defines strategic training and examines how cutting-edge T&D professionals are using training and development as a solution to business and performance problems. In doing so, Wilson relays how a strategic focus can help to promote fad-free training interventions, in order to increase the department's credibility with line management. As an experienced former top executive and strategic training manager in the corporate world, Wilson outlines how to link training interventions to business goals and strategies by conducting appropriate training needs assessments and soliciting genuine participation from management. Throughout, relevant examples and numerous practical insights are discussed to elucidate what can be an abstract idea to some trainers.

Next, the biggest challenges in needs assessment, which is traditionally viewed as the first step in the training process, are addressed. Jennifer Guidry and Janice Simmons, Ph.D., both accomplished training and development professionals, team up to examine how trainers can determine when training is really needed, when training is not the answer, and how to tell the difference. Most importantly, throughout the chapter, Guidry and Simmons contribute examples grounded in actual training scenarios they have confronted in which training was, and in which training was not, the appropriate solution. This is a critical concept for trainers and organizations to grasp in order to avoid creating programs that have little chance of correcting the performance discrepancy at hand.

At this point, Larry Pace, Ph.D., a former training manager in the corporate world and adept consultant in the field, examines the world of technology as related to training. It is obvious that new and fast-changing technologies in the training classroom are a given. But of all these recently emerging delivery and support technologies, what are the distinct characteristics, advantages, and disadvantages of each? Pace discusses this, along with the situations in which these technologies make the most sense to exploit. Numerous relevant examples are discussed to demonstrate the use of leading technologies that help to administer, design, support, and deliver learning in various environments. Such technologies include, but are not limited to, Internet delivery, interactive video, virtual and augmented reality, Intelligent Tutoring Systems, and Electronic Performance Support Systems (EPSS). Finally, decision criteria are outlined to help training professionals determine when these technologies are worth the effort, time, and investment to adopt, and when they are not.

At this point in the book, I explore the vexing problem of training transfer and how to improve employees' use of trained knowledge, skills, and abilities back on the job. Reasons why the transfer problem is oftentimes ignored in organizations are discussed as well as the various factors that influence transfer—before, during, and after training. A field study of a posttraining transfer intervention called relapse prevention is highlighted, along with the study's important implications for trainers. Finally, a simplified framework is advanced for tackling the transfer dilemma, based upon a compilation of tactics and techniques outlined in the training literature. The framework identifies specific and practical actions that trainers, trainees, and managers can invoke (before, during, and after programs) to effectively increase the extent to which trainees use training back on the job. Ultimately, behavioral change is the key to what learning is all about and must never escape our foremost attention.

The next issue in the book has recently showed up on the trainer radar screen; it has been referenced as "performance consulting" and "human performance technology" by various writers (for example, Robinson & Robinson, 1996; Wile, 1996). Regardless of the term, the idea we are talking about in this chapter is a turn toward a holistic approach to training and development, which takes trainers beyond classroom solutions and instead focuses on holistic performance solutions. The author of this chapter, L. Michael Wykes, who skillfully embraces this very perspective and has previously published on the topic, examines the growing trend of focusing on performance solutions versus training programs. In other words, instead of being program developers and instructors, training professionals are fast becoming performance engineers. This broader role for training professionals promises to change the perspective they embrace, the interventions they consider, and the role they play in firms.

In the final portion of the book, we elaborate upon the critical roles trainers assume in organizations. Specifically, Jennifer Guidry makes an encore appearance by penning this last chapter on the varied and increasing number of hats trainers wear in organizations. Traditionally, trainers have assumed some combination (if not all) of the following roles: analysts, designers, facilitators, administrators, event planners, and strategists. Guidry discusses and evaluates these traditional roles and how to execute them for maximum impact. She also introduces three new roles that appear to be surfacing for trainers—change ambassador, internal marketer, and spiritual guide. Jennifer argues that trainers are increasingly becoming the spiritual healers of the workplace, helping people to find meaning and purpose in their work lives and encouraging them to "keep the faith" despite the obstacles faced in today's spiritually bereft organizations. This is a role that clearly needs to be handled delicately, responsibly, and effectively.

FINAL INTRODUCTORY COMMENTS

In summary, the purpose of this book is to examine closely the leading issues and challenges voiced by trainers. The specific issues we address include the following: the strategic linkage of training to firm goals, the determination of training versus nontraining needs, the transfer of training to the job, new training technologies, the growing emphasis on a holistic training perspective, and last, the multiple and increasing number of hats that trainers wear. All of the contributors were carefully chosen, maintain numerous industry connections, possess extensive training and development experience in multiple capacities, and have their finger on the very pulse of training.

What is important to keep in mind before reading the remaining chapters is that, while on the surface these chapters may appear to tap different (and in some cases seemingly unrelated) issues, they are all ultimately interrelated. These interdependencies will become more apparent as each chapter is explored. More importantly, these connections are highlighted in the final chapter because a comprehensive approach to achieving high-impact training practice status will address all issues in this book and their interrelationships.

BIBLIOGRAPHY

Noe, R.A. (1999). *Employee training and development*. Boston: Irwin McGraw-Hill.
Robinson, D.G., & Robinson, J.C. (1996). *Performance consulting: Moving beyond training*. San Francisco: Berrett-Koehler Publishers.
Wile, David. (1996). Why doers do. *Performance & Instruction, 35*, 30–35.

Chapter 2

STRATEGIC TRAINING: CREATING ADVANTAGE AND ADDING VALUE

Joseph V. Wilson III

Listen in on an informal discussion among top executives of competing firms. These leaders are nearing the end of a dinner party at their industry association's annual conference. The topic of conversation for the last ten minutes has been the recent training and development exercises in which they have participated. A lengthy predinner reception has fueled the participants' bravado, and the dinner partners are successively regaling each other with the superiority and uniqueness of their personal experiences.

Jim: Well, our top management team just returned from an incredible time of shooting the white water in Colorado. Talk about a fantastic week. We nearly lost our CEO when he was thrown from the raft and splashed down next to this huge boulder and . . .

Anne: I can't see our leadership group ever participating in an outdoor adventure exercise—it's just not our style—*but* at our last offsite retreat, our CFO had a harrowing *indoor* experience! We hired an industrial psychologist to analyze our personality and leadership styles and to train us on how we could become more effective leaders, managers, and team players. She paired us up explaining that our partners' styles were 180 degrees from our own, that we were miles apart in the ways that we approached problem solving and life for that matter. You should have seen the face of our CFO when he realized that he had been paired with the CEO. . . .

Cal: My most recent training occurred when the IT manager decided that all of the executives (and the whole company for that matter) needed to learn how to use email and LotusNotes. We spent the better part of three days attempting to become proficient with the technology. But guess what? Our CEO won't touch his computer, so most of our work is still done the good old-fashioned way—with mounds of paper. What a waste!

Margaret: At our firm, we wouldn't think of training together. We each choose training and development topics that we believe will benefit our individual careers and performance. Last month, I found this really awesome empowerment seminar in Utah. The skiing was tremendous. I highly recommend it to any of you and your companies.

While admittedly hypothetical, these exchanges provide revealing insights that will not surprise training and development professionals and their firm's leaders. Individuals and organizations can choose from a seemingly endless menu of training and development options. As seen in these examples, a wide range of motivations exist for investing time and dollars in training and development initiatives.

Among the most pressing challenges for those charged with stewardship of an organization's resources are to ensure that investments in training and development are strategically significant. Said another way, effective leaders must expect training and development interventions to make a critical and tangible contribution to the achievement of the enterprise's overall strategy. Throughout the remainder of this chapter, this notion will be referred to and discussed as *strategic training*.

This chapter will examine the underlying meaning of strategic training. It will describe strategic training's potential to create advantage and value in organizations. Recommendations will be presented to enhance the credibility of training and development efforts, as this will discourage organizations from wasting precious resources in pursuit of faddish, nonstrategic interventions. Suggestions will be presented to assist those charged with gaining top management participation and support of training and development initiatives. Finally, two cases will illustrate strategic training's ability to contribute high-impact training results.

ENSURING TRAINING IS REALLY STRATEGIC

In an era where downsizing and expense rationalization efforts are commonplace, the use of the terms *strategy* and *strategic* are on the rise. One motivation for this usage could be the misguided belief that by associating or appending any activity with these terms, they could be viewed as having a higher priority and thus escape a cost cutter's budget ax. As a result, routine supporting activities are increasingly appearing with grandiose monikers such as "strategic" support and "strategic" purchasing.

Training and development professionals are not immune from the cavalier usage of the "s" word—strategy (Hubbard, 2000). As such, it is important to explain clearly what strategic training is, to describe how to determine whether initiatives are strategic, and to present an overview of the strategic training process.

What Is Strategy?

A determination of whether training is strategic must begin with an understanding of the meaning and nature of strategy. Strategy has been traditionally seen as the art and science of generalship to accomplish military objectives. In a more contemporary organizational context, strategy focuses on developing the roadmap for the direction and actions necessary to produce successful performance, for and with customers.

Strategy's chief purpose can be seen as building advantage vis-à-vis competitors, resulting in growing and sustaining leadership and performance (Porter, 1997). In addition, Porter offers that an organization's ability to produce ongoing advantage depends upon the existence of a clear strategy that enables both the creation of significant differentials versus competitors and superior execution.

Other helpful insights include (1) strategy as an enabler of purposeful opportunism (Drucker, 1999), (2) strategy as a form of organizational learning (Mohrman and Mohrman, 1993), and (3) strategy as a systematic and disciplined way of anticipating and evaluating the future (Cross, 2000). To enable opportunism, organizational learning and anticipation of the future, strategy formulation requires significant investments in regimented, advance planning (O'Connell, 1986).

Merging these concepts, strategy will effectively communicate a number of important elements. It will describe a set of performance objectives (optimally, for and with customers), the basis on which an organization will differentiate itself from all other competitors, a compelling sense of how it will capitalize on future opportunities, and a commitment to benefit continuously from the learning gained in the process. Further, to be effective, strategy must be comprehended and embraced by each of its organizational constituencies—customers, shareholders, employees, suppliers, and the communities in which the enterprise operates.

The existence of these elements, and hence, the degree to which any activity, including training and development, is deemed "strategic" can be assessed by considering the ten simple and illuminating questions presented in table 2.1. These questions were assembled (and embellished) from an article based upon interviews with Andrew D. Paparozzi and Mark Tietbohl (Cross, 2000). The degree to which an organization has carefully thought out and communicated meaningful answers to these questions may be a strong indicator of the efficacy of its strategy. Well-crafted strategies carefully address each of these questions.

By asking these ten questions, outsiders and insiders alike can quickly determine the degree to which an organization, division, department or in-

Table 2.1
Questions to Assess Strategic Content

1. Who are our customers?	Who will be targeted? Who will NOT be targeted?
2. How dynamic is our customer base?	How is our attraction and retention of key customers; how rapidly are their needs and demands changing?
3. What will they receive?	What products and services will we deliver?
4. Why will customers choose us?	What will customers perceive as our source of competitive edge?
5. What type of firm are we now?	How do we identify our most important customers and products?
6. What really drives our business?	What is our most significant performance factor—technology, financial prowess, or customer orientation?
7. How will we grow?	Where will we focus for new business—existing or new customers/markets/products?
8. Where will critical resources be procured?	How will we ensure the availability of resources critical to our customers?
9. How dynamic is our employee base?	How is our attraction and retention of key employees; how rapidly are their needs and demands changing?
10. How will we determine "profitability"?	How long will we invest before receiving a return?

Some elements derived from: L. Cross, Planning an effective business strategy (April 2000), *Graphic Arts Monthly*, 62–65.

dividual is strategically focused. Similarly, one can also ascertain the degree to which a particular function, such as training and development, is linked, or "strategic." Inconsistent or omitted responses signal a lack of alignment or the absence of clear strategy and should signal a wake-up call to managers.

Discussing Training in a Strategic Context

The traditional role of training and development has been a supporting one. In this light, training has generally been thought of as enabling strategic achievement. It has been viewed as an element both subordinate to and in support of execution, that is, a tactical intervention providing people with the skills they need to carry out their duties (Hubbard, 2000). The goal of training has been to develop knowledge, skill, and ability competencies that can be routinely and successfully applied (Noe, 1999). Elsewhere, the principal purpose of training has been more broadly described as supporting the short- and long-term strategic goals of the company (Keene, 1991). The success of training that is considered strategic lies in its contribution to organizational effectiveness (O'Connell, 1986).

Given the emphasis on the tactical, supporting nature of training, some strategic planners could be troubled by the combination of the terms *strategic* and *training*. For them, the joint notion of "strategic training" may be discordant or confusing.

Indeed, purists often draw sharp distinctions between strategy and tactics. Drawing again from strategy's military roots, strategy is distinguished from tactics in that it emphasizes planning and coordinating the forces required to achieve a specified objective. Military tactics focus on execution, or the processes and activities associated with the operations of an actual engagement.

The potential for confusion extends beyond strategic planning purists. When considering the ramifications of "strategic" training, other audiences may derive various interpretations from this term. For example, the following three unique possibilities for understanding strategic training can be derived (Catalanello & Redding, 1989):

1. Equipping leaders to understand, plan, and think strategically.
2. Participating in the development of strategic plans (i.e., training and development professionals prominently involved in the strategic planning process).
3. Selecting and delivering training and development initiatives that directly support an organization's strategic plans.

Each of these interpretations could become the singular focus for those considering the meaning and contribution of strategic training. Given the obvious and significant interrelationships among these possibilities, a richer and more precise working definition of strategic training would be helpful. For purposes of this chapter, strategic training and development will be defined in the next section.

Defining Strategic Training

As defined here, strategic training refers to the initiatives that develop employee competencies and produce ongoing differentiation, advantage, and achievement. This working definition can be of immense value to training and development professionals, as well as to leaders and managers, in a wide variety of organizations. It refines and simplifies the broader set of questions seen earlier in table 2.1. This definition can also serve as a swift and powerful evaluation tool for any proposed training and development initiative.

When a training and development initiative is proposed, persons charged with its review and approval can conduct a cursory evaluation with essentially four basic inquiries. The first inquiry focuses on the specific competencies that the initiative proposes to create ("What competencies will the initiative develop?"). This question would be followed with successive inquiries about the manner in which the initiative will produce ongoing differentiation, advantage, and superior performance. ("How will this initiative enable differentiation of the organization versus competitors? How will it enable us to achieve sustainable advantage? How will this initiative produce superior results?"). If the reviewer becomes convinced that the proposed initiative effectively produces value for the organization by creating continuing differentiation, advantage, and performance consistent with the organization's overall objectives, the initiative has earned the right to be deemed "strategic" training.

It will be instructive to recount the strategic training lifecycle. It is not only important to understand what strategic training is and how it can be evaluated, but also to have an appreciation of the steps by which it is conceived, carried out, and ultimately judged. These following six steps are fairly universal in the strategic training process (O'Connell, 1986):

1. *Engage organization leadership*—Top management involvement and buy-in is the first step in the formulation of strategic training initiatives. Absent the wholehearted concurrence and support of an organization's executive cadre at the outset, the effectiveness, and in turn, the strategic value of a proposed initiative will be jeopardized.

2. *Identify strategic objectives*—Borrowing from the questions presented in table 2.1, the sponsor and author of training must exhibit clear understanding of the critical strategic issues that will determine the organization's success. A helpful regimen to ensure that training initiatives address the firm's most important opportunities is to use a formal confirmation or discovery agreement with top management.

3. *Perform a needs analysis*—This step involves documenting the specific competencies needed to facilitate ongoing differentiation, advantage, and achievement. Assessing the present state of these competencies and identifying the gap that must be addressed to become competitively superior is the goal. Chapter 3 provides more comprehensive guidance for carrying out needs assessment efforts.

4. *Procure resources/design interventions*—A range of options is available to the training manager to build the competencies required for organizational success. Internal or external resources can be utilized along with various amalgamations of line and staff personnel and instructional technologies. One of the major contributions of the strategic training process lies in its discipline in selecting the optimal mix of resources to achieve training objectives.

5. *Develop an implementation plan*—Special attention is given to the timing of strategic training implementation to ensure that the highest impact employee audiences (that is, those who can produce the greatest benefit for customers and the organization) receive competency-enhancing training and development early and frequently.

6. *Evaluate success*—Rigorous measurement and accountability for expected results should be a hallmark of strategic training. Learning from successes and failures becomes corporate "know how" or "know how not to" assets.

As a review, strategic training has been defined as those initiatives that develop employee competencies and produce ongoing differentiation, advantage, and achievement. Given this definitional clarity, the next issue examined is how to create advantage and value using strategic training.

CREATING ADVANTAGE AND VALUE WITH STRATEGIC TRAINING

Training and development initiatives that are deemed "strategic" can be significant and, often, unique sources of advantage and value for organizations. This section advances five ways that strategic training contributes to the production of advantage and value, as depicted in figure 2.1. These include: (1) developing essential competencies, (2) creating new knowledge, (3) promoting ongoing learning, (4) facilitating communication and focus, and (5) encouraging change adaptiveness and risk identification.

Developing Essential Competencies

In a volatile and rapidly changing world, strategic opportunism becomes a prerequisite for success. Strategic training focuses on the identification of competencies that will be required to achieve success in the midst of change and in anticipation of it. In this regard, a key contribution of strategic training is to equip leaders with the competencies necessary to perform in the future. Effective leaders of the future will require prowess as (Conger, 1993):

1. *Strategic opportunists*—who quickly locate opportunities that others have missed, primarily on the strength of superior customer understanding.

2. *Global executives*—who can understand and adeptly move in a wide variety of cultures.

3. *Managers of decentralized units*—who coach and coordinate heavier incidences of teams, self-directed units, and independent contractors.

4. *Diversity champions*—who deftly meld multiethnic and varied viewpoints into cohesive purpose and produce superior performance.

5. *Interpersonal role models*—who display exemplary interaction skills and encourage them in others.

6. *Community builders*—who empower and cast compelling visions.

Figure 2.1
Five Ways Strategic Training Can Add Value

These are critical leadership competencies for performance-driven organizations. Such competencies do not appear to be among the native abilities of many leaders. Accordingly, the strategic training process identifies the most important competencies in advance and designs interventions to ensure leaders develop and apply them as a source of advantage.

There are obvious training implications and specific interventions required for each of the six leadership competencies profiled. Given strategic opportunism's significance in the creation of advantage and value, it will be beneficial to identify several training components that can enhance the prospects of producing opportunistic advantage. Conger suggests that strategic opportunism can be stimulated by sending managers into the marketplace, incorporating action learning heavily focused on the leaders' own companies, including maverick insiders or outsiders who can challenge myopic perspectives, involving junior officers in strategic processes earlier in their careers, utilizing new and perhaps experimental learning techniques, and demanding long-term thinking (Conger, 1993).

Creating New Knowledge

A second potential source of strategic training value creation lies in the development of knowledge that is new to the organization, and if the company is fortunate, new to the marketplace as well. Many training organizations major in storing and disseminating old knowledge. Their training and development interventions fail to produce new insights or intellectual capital. Many strategically valuable "new knowledge" products should be expected from well-designed and executed strategic training and development efforts (Coulson-Thomas, 2000). These new products, insights, and breakthroughs, based upon Coulson-Thomas's work, could be generated from training activities and interventions that successfully spark creativity, energy, exploration, inquiry, learning, or discovery. It is these types of activities that can, and often do, produce value-creating ideas and intellectual capital. As illustrated in figure 2.2, strategic training can contribute to building the organization's basis of differentiation, competitive advantage, and achievement by creating "new knowledge."

The relatively recent focus on the heightened criticality of knowledge work (that is, the heightened influence of knowledge as an economic and personal resource) is of particular interest with respect to the creation of advantage and intellectual capital. The more productive knowledge workers

Figure 2.2
Producing New Knowledge with Strategic Training

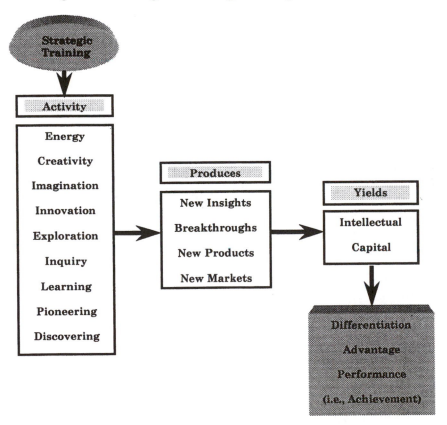

are, the higher the likelihood that they will be able to create valuable intellectual capital. Accordingly, factors affecting knowledge worker productivity will also bear on the strategic training process. While the understanding of the drivers of knowledge worker productivity is not well-developed, the following factors have been identified (Drucker, 1999):

1. Knowledge workers must be continuously asked to clearly identify the tasks for which they are responsible.
2. Knowledge workers must be accountable for their own productivity. They must be fairly autonomous and manage themselves.
3. Knowledge workers must work in an environment that supports ongoing innovation.
4. Knowledge workers need continuous learning and opportunities to teach others.
5. Knowledge worker productivity must be as concerned with quality as it is with quantity.
6. Knowledge workers must be viewed and treated as assets (not costs), and organizations must engender employees' desires to want to work for it.

Training interventions for knowledge workers must incorporate these factors. Strategic training initiatives must be knowledge worker friendly. In other words, they must be clearly defined, permitting autonomous activity, and supportive of continuous innovation and quality, with opportunities to learn and to teach along the way. Knowledge workers create intellectual capital when they generate innovation, improvement, and redesigned ideas. Designing training that develops and supports these competencies is challenging (Mohrman & Mohrman, 1993).

Strategic training must also incorporate elements of culture and environment that are conducive to the manufacture of intellectual capital into interventions. Mohrman and Mohrman suggest that where there are certain ongoing activities there is a greater likelihood of being successful in developing and applying innovation, improvement, and redesigned competencies to create advantage through intellectual capital. Their cited activities include, but are not limited to the following:

- leadership communicating a clear strategy
- extensive organizational communication
- inter-functional cooperation and shared goals
- strong orientation to both internal and external customers
- all stakeholders participating in design
- emphasis and value of continuous reassessment
- open information sharing
- structures viewed as temporary and changing

Training and development organizations should be based upon and espouse similar values and activities as outlined by Mohrman and Mohrman. Specifically, training professionals must formulate, articulate, and communicate their mission; seek cross-organizational input; be consumed by internal and external customer needs; solicit multistakeholder involvement throughout the training process; evaluate initiatives for continuous improvement; and modify their departmental structure flexibly to meet organizational needs. By doing so, training can play an important role in supporting the creation of new knowledge and advantage for organizations.

Promoting Ongoing Learning

Strategic training is by its nature a learning process. Learning can become a source of advantage as it improves retention, cost-effectiveness, and organizational speed (Ruggles, 1998). Learning has historically been the domain of training departments serving up a menu of current business, technical, and organizational instruction, each of which may have questionable value to the success of organizations in rapidly changing competitive environments (Baldwin, Danielson, & Wiggenhorn, 1997). These authors hold that in changing marketplaces, strategic learning must move more of its emphasis from employee development and current business needs to creating skills in building new businesses and redefining old ones. In short, they believe that leaders must be equipped to learn their way through challenges and opportunities at an accelerating pace.

In this view, it is the ability to learn on the fly that creates advantage. Learning leaders and organizations can face a wide range of situations and problems, confident that they can learn faster and out maneuver competitors. While the distance between creating new knowledge and being able to learn advantageously may be small, the distinction is a valid one.

Facilitating Communication and Focus

The strategic training process can also serve as a mechanism to promote organizational communication and focus. Training interventions can provide a unique platform to support horizontal and vertical integration within organizations (Watad & Ospina, 1999). The interactions of employees from various units and levels can foster organizational effectiveness and efficiency through strengthened relationships, networks and knowledge of available resources.

Watad and Ospina identify four conditions necessary for training to play a successful integrative role:

1. *Senior management must be involved* at the outset, throughout, and afterward.
2. *Training must be positioned as a positive opportunity* where those with the motivation and ability to apply learning hone their skills.

3. *Training must be identified as one part of an overarching development plan in support of the organization's strategic objectives* as a component of an ongoing (not one-time) set of development experiences of obvious importance to the organization's success.

4. *Training must facilitate continuing processes to diminish conflict and stimulate communication across competing departmental interests* launching mutually beneficial relationships that can survive and ultimately break down barriers impeding total organization performance.

These authors further suggest that training is strategic when it becomes developmental in nature, capitalizing on every opportunity to enhance learning and prolong the integration achieved.

Encouraging Change Adaptiveness and Risk Identification

Two final benefits of strategic training are also notable. First, strategic training is a continuous process. It is not an event! The most successful strategic training often incorporates its tenets in the day-to-day disciplines of the organization. When this occurs, the organization becomes adept at identifying and capitalizing on change, both customer-initiated change and change instituted from within the company (Hussey, 1999).

Second, strategic training heightens organizational risk awareness. Strategic training promotes the understanding of the relative simplicity of training employees to handle new products or technology as compared to preparing them for new businesses or changed ways (Adams, 1999). As such, strategic training assesses and reveals some of the risk elements inherent in pursuing novel strategies.

BUILDING STRATEGIC TRAINING CREDIBILITY

It happens in September, October, and November each year. As the leaves begin to fall from the trees, it is a safe bet that CFOs' budget axes are falling at thousands of performance-driven companies. When the dreaded, but fully expected, review process reaches its third or fourth round and projected earnings are still significantly below the targets set at the beginning of budget season, the "usual suspects are rounded up." The "usual suspects" typically include expenses such as marketing, training and development, travel and entertainment, consulting, and maintenance. It is usually only a matter of time before they (or some portion of them) are eliminated from the budgets.

In previous rounds, line managers have valiantly defended these expenses as important supporting elements of their business plans. Now, when pressures to improve the bottom line intensify, they begin to make painful tradeoff decisions. Will they raise their revenue growth estimates, reduce "line *and* staff" expenses, or some combination of the two? Most participants in this stage of budget negotiations can predict the likely outcome. Managers scramble to develop new support plans absent a significant portion of the funding previously deemed necessary for budget achievement initiatives!

Training and development professionals cringe and experience frustration when they witness their vital initiatives become classified as "discretionary" expenses and end up on the budget chopping block. They question the business judgment of the line managers who accede to these cuts: "Don't they realize how short-sighted they are to cut training and development? Don't they understand that their people won't be equipped to succeed without the training initiatives? New employee competencies are the linchpin of their strategy and business plan, are they crazy or what? Training and development is just an easy mark when it comes to expense reductions. They will be sorry—they are hurting themselves in the long run to go for short-term gains."

Still, it happens year after year in many organizations. Training and development investments often do not survive later round budget reviews. What can training and development professionals do to enhance the odds that training initiatives stay alive in budgets and create advantage and value for these companies? In other words, how can training's credibility be improved? The answer lies, at least partially, in beginning to position training as a relevant, strategic, and significant contributor to success. Perhaps a practical experiment will illuminate this point.

Imagine a line manager looking for reference material to enhance her knowledge of efficacious training. She starts by visiting a prominent national bookstore. After locating the business management section, she hones in on the human resources or personnel subsection. What categories of books will she find?

There are a number of titles dealing with motivating and rewarding employees. Others concern recruiting, hiring, firing, and employee law. And yes, after looking carefully, she sees a few books focused on training. It doesn't take long to observe that a number of the books in the training category have titles emphasizing words such as *games, fun,* and *icebreakers.* Are games and fun what training is all about? No. But it is possible that resources of this nature fuel prevailing perceptions contributing to the credibility crisis training and development professionals face.

To survive the rigors of the budget process and be viewed as a more significant component of a line manager's business plans, training and development leaders must dramatically increase their effectiveness in communicating the credibility and contribution of their initiatives! Just how can they accomplish this? The next section examines six major actions for building strategic training credibility as summarized in table 2.2.

Table 2.2
Building Credibility for Strategic Training

Align	• Involve top management
	• Employ strategic thinking
Position	• Focus on benefits
	• Customers
	• Organization
	• Employees
	• Emphasize performance
	• Demonstrate strategic fit
Learn	• Check reality
	• Involve customers
	• Leverage past lessons
Prioritize	• Categorize by impact
	• Ensure consistency
Measure	• Quantify expectations
	• Evaluate results
Avoid	• Sidestep fads
	• Avoid inaccurate estimates
	• Prevent prior mistakes

Aligning Strategic Training Initiatives with Organizational Objectives

First and foremost, training and development initiatives must be aligned and inextricably linked to the achievement of the organization's business plan. While it is difficult to find articles that neglect mention of this cardinal principle, it is a rare occurrence to find line managers who are passionately convinced that their business development plans will be in serious jeopardy if training and development initiatives are eliminated or significantly cut back.

This phenomenon suggests that practitioners must do a better job of involving and investing line managers in the development of strategic training initiatives (and a later section in this chapter will offer specific suggestions). To gain credibility, the dialogue between training and development leaders and line managers must be denominated in strategic thinking. Their interactions and common language must exhibit three components.

The major components of strategic thinking, according to William Marrinam, President of Marrinam Associates, Raleigh, North Carolina, include: (1) focus, (2) flexibility, and (3) distillation (Cross, 2000). Focus consists of the ability to identify the things an organization does best, particularly for and with customers. Flexibility is the ability to envision possible future occurrences and a range of responses that are likely to produce success. Distillation involves pinpointing the factors that will have the greatest impact on the organization's success.

When line managers observe training and development professionals delivering initiatives that build on what the organization does best, anticipating and preparing for future scenarios, and addressing factors with the greatest impact on the business, training credibility will be greatly enhanced. Line managers will be more committed to strategic training initiatives because they mirror their own values and priorities.

Strategic training initiatives will gain further credibility when training leaders appropriately and objectively assess and communicate the relative priorities of the various efforts and programs comprising the strategic training program. By proactively informing line managers of the priority categorization and potential impacts of each training initiative, optimization decisions in the allocation of scarce resources can be made more judiciously.

A helpful and easy-to-use method for assigning a training initiative's priority identifies a training investment as falling within one of the following categories (Hussey, 1999):

1. meets needs that have a significant, immediate impact on performance
2. meets needs yielding long-term performance
3. meets needs or desires of employees that have less certain impact on performance

By prioritizing investments in this or some similar manner, training and development managers can demonstrate objectivity and gain additional credibility. One caution, however, about applying Hussey's categorization. In a tight labor market, especially for knowledge workers, there is a danger that training and development important to these workers' productivity and their retention could fall largely in the last priority category. This is especially true when there is no discernible impact on organizational performance in the near term. For example, technology-focused employees' zeal to stay current on new developments may not be seen as critical to next year's plan achievement. Failure to provide leading-edge exposure may lead to future unpreparedness or loss of these employees to a competitor, particularly if they sense that their skills and market value will be impaired by not staying up to date. Since the last priority category is easiest for line managers to cut, care should be taken to ensure that critical initiatives important to knowledge workers be clearly identified and preserved.

While it is essential for training professionals to understand the credibility enhancement potential available by proactively prioritizing initiatives, line managers should also be aware of the erosion of credibility that occurs within the organization when training and development investments are not a consistent, high-priority activity. It has been suggested that from a strategic point of view, there are only two types of training and development activities—those that consistently deliver and are a long term, high priority and those that are not (Hubbard, 2000).

Inconsistent training and development periods of emphasis (for example, this year it's in the budget and next year it's out) send conflicting and detrimental messages to the employees in an organization. The level and nature of an organization's training and development activity speaks loudly about how it values employees (Keene, 1991). The credibility of strategic training initiatives is certainly impacted by the degree to which they have been consistently offered.

Positioning Strategic Training as a Performance Enhancer

Strategic training's credibility is also affected by its positioning within a given organization. In many organizations, training and development initiatives are viewed through a cost or expense avoidance lens. Oddly enough, even in such organizations, the direct, much less indirect, cost of training is seldom evaluated (that is, time away and opportunity costs are usually overlooked). Training and development credibility and effectiveness can be enhanced by placing more emphasis on the benefits that initiatives deliver in improving the organization's performance (Hussey, 1999).

Specifying what benefits will accrue to whom is a fundamental requirement for credible strategic training. Being clear about the benefits that will be delivered to each of the following audiences is paramount. As outlined in figure 2.3, trainers should delineate how customers, the organization, and employees will benefit. In other words, three simple acronyms can guide this process: (1) WIIFC (what's in it for customers?), (2) WIIFO (what's in it for the organization?), and (3) WIIFE (what's in it for the employees?).

Perhaps the most important role strategic training can play is to be a facilitator of and a valuable contributor to an organization's ongoing performance enhancement process. For some trainers, this role will require a dramatic shift in focus from training needs to performance needs. In this context, the definitions of terms commonly used by training and development personnel must change and be reflected as follows (Peterson, 1998):

- *Training need*—A human performance requirement best dealt with by training.

- *Training need identification*—The activity that attempts to inventory training needs (both organization and individual).

- *Performance assessment*—The determination of performance problems inhibiting on-the-job performance and appropriate solutions.

Figure 2.3
Positioning Strategic Training

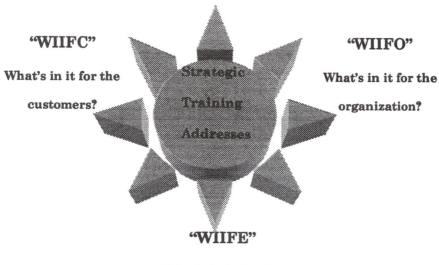

"WIIFC"

What's in it for the

customers?

Strategic
Training
Addresses

"WIIFO"

What's in it for the

organization?

"WIIFE"

What's in it for the

employees?

An additional positioning aspect that can enhance the credibility of strategic training is to ensure that it is seen as important in the context of the organization's overall strategic fit. The individual and collective skills that an organization needs are highly interrelated with six other elements. As set forth in the well-known McKinsey 7S framework, each of seven elements is connected to and a derivative of the others—strategy, structure, systems, shared values, style, staff, and skills (Waterman, 1982). Strategic training should be positioned and understood as an integral part of the total strategic framework, not as a stand-alone consideration for budget cuts.

A related role of strategic training is to clearly identify when training and development initiatives are *not* the optimal solution for improving an organization's performance. The strategic training process must routinely pose the question "Is there a better, nontraining business solution that will enable goal achievement?" Training may not effectively address certain performance challenges, for example, when problems have roots in environmental issues such as poor leadership, lack of motivation, missing information and tools, or nonexistent rewards. Chapters 3 and 6 will expand greatly upon this important insight.

To summarize, trainers must position initiatives as performance enhancers and benefit creators. When strategic training initiatives are clearly aligned with business objectives and understood in the context of their fit within the overall strategy of the firm, credibility will increase.

Leveraging Learning

Ensuring that certain learnings are incorporated into training process design and delivery can further increase the credibility afforded strategic training. Two important learning considerations are experimentation and leveraging past learning.

How often are major training initiatives proposed and rolled out in organizations without having been subjected to substantive field or pilot testing? The answer—more often than training and development professionals or managers may want to admit. When this situation occurs and outcomes are not as expected, training and development initiative credibility is negatively impacted.

One standard component of military training has been the use of expensive, large-scale war games. At the conclusion of the games, various ideas and assumptions are developed and recorded to improve future performance. However, even massively expensive exercises do not produce a fully authentic environment or reliable conclusions since the simulations still fall far short of real-life combat experience. Accordingly, military trainers are making increasing use of experiments to determine the validity of game/simulation outcome lessons in realistic combat situations (Scott, 1998).

For nonmilitary organizations, experimentation is much less costly and reality is easier to replicate. In fact, the most impactful experimentation available to organizations might involve inviting external customers to participate in the development and perhaps even the delivery of training initiatives. Surprisingly, customers are a missing component of many firms' planning processes (Cross, 2000).

Borrowing further from the strategic planning discipline, it has been suggested that planners often overlook issues and lessons from past plans and fail to conduct careful analyses of factors that contributed to performance shortfalls (Oliver, 2000). How many training and development managers conduct a review of the past five years' initiatives (how and why they succeeded, how and why they fell short of expectations, and so on) and include the learned lessons as part of the introduction to their future years' plans? My suspicion and personal experience is that disciplined use of this important source of learning is rare.

Historical analyses of this sort demonstrate a willingness to be accountable and evidence of careful underwriting for proposed initiatives and interventions. As such, initiative credibility is enhanced.

Measuring Strategic Training Contributions

Perhaps the most important contributor to the credibility of strategic training comes from a measurement and evaluation component. Objective comparison of the actual outcomes achieved by strategic training to those projected can greatly add to the credibility of training and development initiatives.

For performance measures to be of worth, two questions must be answered. Why should initiatives be measured and what kinds of measurements should be tracked? Measurements should be undertaken to synchronize all of the elements of mission, strategy and employee behaviors in order to focus on and improve the most important organizational activities and to provide a quantitative definition for success (Lawton, 2000). Lawton cites three types of measures warranting tracking:

- customer-desired outcomes
- customer-desired products
- processes that customers experience

It is interesting to note that all of these measures are termed in customer activity and, moreover, are indications of how well customer needs are being met. Given organizations' increasing outlay for people and their training and development, the magnitude of dollars invested is coming under heightened scrutiny. Just as a new computer system or real estate purchase would require rigorous return on investment analysis, so, too, should training and development activities.

Traditionally, training programs have been subjected to two forms of evaluation (Noe, 1999):

- Formative—ongoing evaluation that is focused on training process improvement. (Is the program administered well? Do the graphics, videos, exercises, and/or music enhance learning? Is the program easy to move through and logical during the pilot run?)
- Summative—posttraining evaluation concerned with the degree of change exhibited by trainees as a result of the training. (Are trainees more productive? Has the safety record improved? Are employees' work skills improved?)

Even more important, though, is the effectiveness of training as measured by the impact it has had on the results of the business. (Are there more new customers? Is the company getting a larger share of customers business? Are customers being treated better? Has the retention of our best customers increased?) Meaningful training and development measurements should directly integrate customer-denominated performance.

One financial services firm seeking to imbed this notion in its employees consistently reiterated it in every internal communication. For this company, each thought process began and ended with customers at the fore-front. The same approach should apply to training and development measures—they should all be connected to customer outcomes.

If the goal of training and development is to improve employee productivity and to deliver advantage and value (for and with customers), what sorts of employee competencies should exist and be evaluated? To create value for customers, employees (and their training) must possess an appreciation of the factors influencing performance—a desire to perform and a set of enabling skills and competencies. The following employee competencies have been suggested to produce superior performance (Zwell & Ressler, 2000):

- *Quality*—The on-going attention and inspection of all critical processes.
- *Flexibility*—The speed of and positive reaction to change.
- *Influence*—The ability to align, persuade, and motivate.
- *Initiative*—The anticipatory identification and handling of challenges and opportunities.   ᛫
- *Integrity*—The building of trust and accountability in relationships.
- *Service orientation*—The commitment to exceeding expectations for customers (both internal and external).
- *Teamwork*—The facilitation and support of employees' cooperative efforts.
- *Results orientation*—The consuming desire to set and achieve significant goals.

Zwell and Ressler indicate that these and other factors contribute to the formation of human capital and claim that an organization's human capital component can contribute up to 30 percent of its market value. But aren't the aforementioned factors difficult to measure? Absolutely. However, given the criticality of measurement, the challenge of operationalizing each of these competencies in customer-centric metrics warrants the undertaking. The yield of such an effort—proper focus and heightened credibility—is worth the attempt.

While it might be argued that a value measurement would be difficult to derive, nearly every business and division learns to measure what it deems to be important. So should it be with strategic training. Not only would joint ownership of a value-created measurement strengthen credibility, it would also discourage frivolous training and development investment and facilitate management buy-in from the outset.

In the final analysis, the most critical question asks whether training and development initiatives enhanced performance. Performance is simply the sum total of the actions taken by people to make an organization function and how well the actions were carried out (Reinhart, 2000). When strategic training is determined to be the best answer to support improved performance, it is imperative that line managers participate in (and own) the designation of the posttraining measurements, which will be used to assess training effectiveness. An attempt should be made to identify new value created as a result of the strategic training initiative, and the line manager and the training manager should share responsibility for the creation of this value.

Avoiding Fads and Common Training Mistakes

The final step to building credibility for strategic training involves avoiding training and development fads and common training mistakes. Being pragmatic in the assessment of "new wave" training contribution potential and sidestepping frequent training pitfalls are both important for training and development professionals' credibility.

Training providers often feel compelled to offer programs that reflect the hottest management strategy and guru fads. In trainers' defense, these offerings are often demanded by the top managers they serve (Ashkenas, 1994). By definition, strategic training should remain centered on competencies that will create differentiation, advantage, and achievement. Alternatively, investing resources in nonstrategic offerings cannot distract managers and trainers.

Remaining centered on initiatives supportive of the organization's strategic training focus will not be easy. Consider the hypothetical example of a training manager fighting for the budget to support the most important objectives of her company. Her CEO sees an article about an opportunity for the executive team to attend a training course that teaches them to drive FormulaFords at over 200mph on a closed racetrack. While the stated objective of the training is to enhance the executives' competitiveness and ability to think and react quickly to handle adversity (Mickey, 1993), she suspects that a primary motivator is the CEO's love of the sport of racing. He suggests that she should make room in her already overtaxed budget for a sizable expenditure to cover this training. Is this a rare or normal occurrence? In some organizations it is rare; but in others, it is encountered rather frequently. The determining factor is the degree of strategic focus, discipline, and stewardship in the organization.

Surprisingly, some training managers consistently undermine their own effectiveness by not learning from the training mistakes that they or their colleagues have commonly made. If any department within an organization should be a learning organization that profits from past experience and industry benchmarks, it should be the training and development group, but this is not always the case. Those who do not incorporate these lessons into future plans often find themselves in a downward spiral of shrinking credibility and funding. The reasons for this occurrence and possible remedies may be found in the following list of "foolish things trainers do" (Shank, 1998). While some of these insights reiterate themes found elsewhere in the present chapter (and throughout the book), explicitly outlining them here will serve to reinforce sound, value-creating training practices. They include the following:

- *Failure to understand the business*—The starting and ongoing point of concentration for strategic trainers is a deep knowledge of the critical drivers of the business.

- *Failure to involve the right people*—Top management buy-in is of utmost importance as discussed further in the next section.

- *Chasing fads*—Training must stay focused on the actions that will build the competencies set forth in the strategic plan. Don't drift. Expect tight linkage to business and measurable results from training investments.

- *Failure to engage participants*—Trainers must ensure that those being trained are fully aware of the training's benefits for customers, the organization, and themselves and engender commitment to realize the expected benefits for all three.

- *Training exclusively (believing training solves every problem)*—Trainers must be discriminating to a fault, ensuring that every manager in the organization understands that the proclamation of "I need some training" will not trigger an automatic training solution.

GAINING TOP MANAGEMENT SUPPORT

Because top management understanding, commitment, and support of strategic training is vital to success, some helpful ideas about gaining and maintaining buy-in are necessary. Scott Parry, founder and chair of Training House of Princeton, New Jersey, suggests ten ways to ensure top management support of training. The following three ideas are especially important to ensuring a strategic training focus and its success (Parry, 1997):

- *Begin at the top*—Become strategic partners with the leaders of the organization's businesses, focusing on delivering competencies that will enhance their performance on critical success factors.

- *Brief managers*—Make sure the managers of those being trained are involved before (that is, create objectives and training preparation), during (that is, tangible support and encouragement of employees in training), and after sessions (that is, reinforcement, motivation and measurement of learning and feedback). This approach will also help to enhance training transfer, which will be discussed more in chapter 5.

- *Document successes*—Identify and market the outcomes and accomplishments of training initiatives within the organization to create opportunities for further performance improvement.

A final way to gain support is to keep top management apprised of successful and unsuccessful strategic training initiatives of competitors via benchmarking. This analysis must go beyond traditional comparisons of training budgets, staff complement, or ratios such as training dollars to sales. To be valuable and credible, this analysis must present a comparison of strategies pursued, the nature and amount of training employed, and an estimate (however rough) of the benefits and value created. By involving top management as strategic partners and objectively assessing training initiatives (including comparisons with competitors and targeted benchmark companies), the probability of gaining management buy-in training will be greatly enhanced. The process for producing well-crafted strategic training starts at the top.

TWO CASES: ACHIEVING HIGH IMPACT WITH STRATEGIC TRAINING

The following two cases grew out of my first-hand experience. Each demonstrates the power and performance-enhancing contribution of strategic training. The first case describes a successful regional bank. The insights shared come from my perspective as an executive for several different groups within the bank during the period described, including the role of director of corporate development responsible for strategy, training, and development.

The second case describes the effects of an international consulting firm's strategic training, as experienced by its client (the bank). My reflections in the second case are the product of having served as the bank's chief liaison with the consulting firm during its multiyear engagement.

Case 1: A Regional Bank

It happened quite unexpectedly. The CFO of a regional bank learned that his boss had suffered a massive heart attack. A few days later, he became the surprise choice of the board of directors to succeed the bank's former CEO.

The bank was abuzz with speculation about the changes that the "new sheriff in town" would institute. During his tenure as CFO, this executive had gained a well-deserved reputation for disciplined cost control and rigorous financial analysis. Most of the organization braced for the inevitable tightening of existing financial controls.

To the shock of most internal observers, the newly elected CEO's first major communication with the bank's staff was that his highest initial priority would be to dramatically enhance the firm's customer orientation. An organization steeped in rules, regulations, procedures, internal focus, and expense control initially received this communiqué without fully appreciating its impact.

As the employees would eventually learn (and many would participate in its development), the firm's new statement of direction would reflect three priorities in addition to its commitment to being market-driven and customer-oriented. They included (1) superior returns for shareholders, (2) quality (particularly in the selection and development of personnel), and (3) investments in the communities the bank served.

One of the most difficult challenges for the company would involve its employee competencies. The employee competencies required to become customer-oriented were radically different from those that had produced past results. The CEO recognized that his employees would require sets of groundbreaking knowledge, skills, and abilities to anticipate customer needs and to proactively meet them. This represented a "sea of change" for a banking organization accustomed to a rigid command and control culture.

So where did the CEO begin when faced with the prospect of building dramatically new competencies? In this case, he commissioned a high profile, multidisciplinary task force that reported directly to him. Its mission was to identify every barrier to serving customers excellently and to propose and implement initiatives to create competitively superior customer orientation. Members of the task force came from every level of the organization. The life span of the task force was several years. It remained the catalyst for customer advocacy until the CEO was convinced that customer orientation had been embraced throughout the bank.

There were a number of key contributors to the company's achieving competitively superior customer orientation. However, chief among them was a strategic training component that ensured the development of customer-focused competencies.

From the outset of its work, the task force identified vital customer-demanded competencies that the bank could deliver while earning desirable returns. The first major training initiative the task force sponsored taught every bank employee how to be consultative and relationship-oriented. This training addressed interactions with fellow workers as well as customers and was tailored for each unit by an outside vendor.

The tenets of these interventions served as the foundation for a stream of consistently higher quality and more tightly focused training and development initiatives over a period of fifteen years. By the end of the period (at which time the bank was acquired), a full range of customer focused, competency-building interventions were offered to employees through a number of channels. The bank employed varying training methods, including an in-house university, subject matter experts, outside training vendors, computer-based training, distance learning, and outside seminars and schools—all designed to support strategically significant customer-focused competencies.

In its last years before acquisition, the bank incorporated two unique and, heretofore, somewhat controversial parties in its training interventions for employees handling high value customers. Several customers and direct competitors were invited to conduct training designed to prepare the employees for an even more valuable role as proactive customer advisors.

As a result of the CEO's leadership and consistent support of strategic training initiatives, the bank prospered. It had become the market share and profitability leader in its markets; its share price had significantly out-performed the S&P 500 Index; and it rewarded its shareholders with an at-tractive premium upon sale. Upon reflection, this CEO attributed much of the success to the employees' sharp focus and performance for customers. Underlying this focus and performance were customer-focused competen-cies wrought by strategic training. In turn, the bank could then deliver dif-ferentiated customer focus and service that created competitive advantage and resulted in the achievement of superior returns to its shareholders.

Case 2: An International Consulting Firm

In the mid-1990s, a regional financial services company recognized that it could no longer successfully compete in its dynamically changing mar-ketplace. Revenue growth was slowing and the company's expense base was not. Its leaders realized that it could not continue to conduct business in the same manner as it had in the past.

The company's executive team was keenly aware of a number of com-petitors' highly touted reengineering efforts. They decided to investigate the reengineering phenomenon to determine if it offered promise and to avoid being "left behind" in a competitively inferior position. The execu-tive team also knew that the company did not possess the expertise or re-sources to pursue this endeavor alone. Accordingly, they decided to engage a consulting firm partner to assist them. Each of the senior managers of the firm was asked to recommend potential consulting firms for consideration. The candidates' list quickly became a "Who's who" of the nation's most highly regarded consulting firms.

Fifteen consulting firms received requests for proposals for an ongoing engagement to identify and support value-creating reengineering oppor-tunities. Twelve firms returned formal proposals bidding for the work. Six of the twelve were invited to make oral presentations to the senior manage-ment team (consisting of fifteen individuals). At the conclusion of the pre-sentations, all but one senior manager agreed that the proposal of Bain & Company, headquartered in Boston, Massachusetts, was superior. As a re-sult, Bain was awarded the company's business and initiated what would grow into a multiyear, multimillion dollar relationship.

Each of the competing consulting firms had excellently communicated their consultants' credentials, described trademarked reengineering and strategy formulation processes, cited successes and testimonials from a wide variety of clients, and displayed deep working experience in the fi-nancial services industry. What then set the chosen proposal and presentation apart? What enabled them to win the business, even though they were not the low cost bidders in a field of highly professional competitors?

The answer—Bain uniquely and powerfully focused on the financial services firm's *customers*, not internal processes. They began by demonstrating a comprehensive understanding of profitable customers' needs, identified what those customers valued, and specified actions that would be necessary to attract and retain them. Each Bain team member reinforced this focus. They suggested that the primary sources of performance improvement for the firm lay in developing superior customer knowledge and delivering exceptional products and services developed from that knowledge. They believed design of the company's internal processes (reengineering) should be secondary and supportive of delivering valuable propositions to customers. Customer processes that created value would receive additional investment and attention. Processes that failed to add value to customers or were inefficient would be rationalized or jettisoned.

Charles Farkas is a Bain director and was a member of the team that made the winning proposal. In a recent interview, Farkas explained that the most important theme within Bain is customer focus—finding and communicating accurate and honest answers for clients that will add value for their activities. Since customers are important to Bain, they believe that their client's customers are important as well. (C. Farkas, personal communication, July 27, 2000).

Everything Bain does serves to reinforce this focus. The company tests potential consultants for the "customer focus instinct" in the hiring process. The first messages delivered to new consultants joining the firm emphasize the criticality of developing compelling customer insights (about Bain's clients and about its clients' customers). Entry-level training builds skills to support this focus, and further formal training enhances the ability of company personnel to excel at developing actionable customer insights.

The internal training objectives at Bain differ from many firms. Their training is not designed to build progressively higher levels of competence in particular technical skills. Instead, their training is geared to producing broader sets of generalizable skills leading to expertise in strategy formulation. Consultants learn how to ask questions, how to look for facts and identify patterns, and solve problems by creating answers and an action plan for clients.

While there is an important formal training component at certain career intervals, Bain ensures a steady diet of customer focus by expecting each consultant to train and share customer perspectives with colleagues in their daily interactions. Leaders also incorporate customer focus into their speeches and communications both inside and outside of the firm. This consulting company seeks to capitalize on every opportunity to inculcate the firm with customer focus. Customer focus is deemed to be a core competence of the firm.

In summary, Bain's consuming focus on customers grows out of a set of concentrated, repetitive emphases—leader communications, on-the-job, and formal training all geared toward creating a distinctive capability—a customer focus core competence. In this sense, strategic training at this consulting firm can be seen throughout the fabric of the entire organization. Strategic training is not seen as the sole purview of the training department. It is far more pervasive. Strategic training in Bain & Co. is the sum of the firm's efforts to create more value for clients and their customers.

CONCLUDING REMARKS

Given the advent of the information age and a forward environment of accelerating change, employee competencies that produce ongoing differentiation, advantage, and achievement will be of utmost importance to competitive organizations. Strategic training initiatives can develop these competencies. To ensure that employee competencies deliver value, training and development professionals must possess and communicate a richer understanding of a strategic focus, enhance the credibility of their initiatives, and become strategic partners with top management. By doing so, strategic training will create ongoing value for organizations, their employees, and their customers.

BIBLIOGRAPHY

Adams, M. (1999, February). Training employees as partners. *HR Magazine*, 64–70.

Ashkenas, R.N. (1994). Beyond fads: How leaders drive change with results. *Human Resource Planning, 17*, 25–45.

Baldwin, T.T., Danielson, C., & Wiggenhorn, W. (1997). The evolution of learning strategies in organizations: From employee development to business redefinition. *The Academy of Management Executive, 11*, 47–58.

Catalanello, R., & Redding, J. (1989). Three strategic training roles. *Training and Development Journal, 43(12)*, 51–55.

Conger, J.A. (1993). The brave new world of leadership training. *Organizational Dynamics, 21(3)*, 46–58.

Coulson-Thomas, C. (2000, May). Send in the clones. *Director*, pp. 34–35.

Cross, L. (2000, April). Planning an effective business strategy. *Graphic Arts Monthly*, 62–65.

Drucker, P.F. (1999). *Management challenges for the 21st century.* New York: HarperBusiness.

Hubbard, A. (2000, February). Training as a strategy and a tactic. *Mortgage Banking*, p. 94.

Hussey, D. (1999). *Strategy and planning: A manager's guide.* Chicester, England: John Wiley & Sons, Ltd.

Keene, M.R. (1991). *The training investment: Banking on people for superior results.* Homewood, IL: Business One Irwin.

Lawton, R. (2000). Using measures to connect strategy with customers. *The Journal for Quality and Participation, 23,* 54–58.

Mickey, R.J. (1993). Road warriors. *The Journal of Business Strategy, 14,* 62–63.

Mohrman, S.A., & Mohrman, A., Jr. (1993). Organizational change and learning. In J.R. Galbraith & E.E. Lawler III and Associates (Eds.), *Organizing for the future: The new logic for managing complex organizations* (pp. 89–107). San Francisco: Jossey-Bass Publishers.

Noe, R.A. (1999). *Employee training and development.* Boston: Irwin McGraw-Hill.

O'Connell, D.J. (1986, August). A six-step program for strategic OA training. *Today's Office,* 44–45.

Oliver, R.W. (2000). A thousand year strategic plan. *The Journal of Business Strategy, 21,* 7–9.

Parry, S.B. (1997). 10 ways to get management buy-in. *Training and Development Journal, 51(9),* 20–22.

Peterson, R. (1998). *Training needs assessment: Meeting the training need for improved performance.* (2nd ed.). London: Kogan Page.

Porter, M. (1997). Creating tomorrow's advantage. In R. Gibson (Ed.), *Rethinking business, principles, competition, control & complexity, leadership, markets and the world* (pp. 49–50). London: Nicolas Brealy Publishing.

Reinhart, C. (2000). How to leap over barriers to performance. *Training and Development Journal, 54(1),* 20–24.

Ruggles, R. (1998). The state of the notion: Knowledge management in practice. *California Management Review, 40,* 80–91.

Scott, W.B. (1998, November 2). Reality checks boost wargame credibility. *Aviation Week & Space Technology,* 63.

Shank, P. (1998). No R-E-S-P-E-C-T? Five foolish things trainers do. *Training and Development Journal, 52(8),* 14–15.

Watad, M., & Ospina, S. (1999). Integrated managerial training: A program for strategic management development. *Public Personnel Management, 28,* 185–196.

Waterman, R.H. (1982). The seven elements of strategic fit. *The Journal of Business Strategy, 2,* 69–73.

Zwell, M., & Ressler, R. (2000). Powering the human drivers of financial performance. *Strategic Finance, 81,* 40–45.

Chapter 3

Needs Assessment: Analyzing Performance Issues and Determining Solutions

Jennifer W. Guidry and Janice L. Simmons

Training and development professionals are frequently invited into situations after clients have already determined that they want training. It makes sense—when they want food, they go to a restaurant. When they want training, they go to a training department. But training professionals often need to help their clients understand that training is a means to an end, and not an end in itself (Mager, 1992). That is, the end in the present context is performance—what people actually do on the job to contribute to the achievement of the organization's goals. Providing training—helping people learn how to do something new or to do something differently—does not guarantee that their on-the-job performance will improve!

Therefore, when training professionals are invited to provide a training solution, they must begin with a *performance assessment* to determine what the performance problems are and what performance solutions may be appropriate, so that "doers" will be more likely to "do" once back on the job (Wile, 1996). If training is determined to be an appropriate solution, a *training needs assessment* must then occur. A training needs assessment includes analyzing the targeted audience, the content that should be covered, and the organizational factors that will impact the training.

To assist clients more effectively, training professionals should be mindful of their biases and avoid suggesting a training solution when, in fact, it will not resolve the performance problem at hand. Certain probing questions may be helpful in any needs analysis effort as illustrated in table 3.1 and discussed throughout the remainder of this chapter.

We will first discuss how to conduct a performance analysis, then how to conduct a training needs assessment. Case studies—including internal consulting and external consulting scenarios—will also be presented to demonstrate how these assessment tools have been used in real-life situations.

PERFORMANCE ASSESSMENT

So why don't "doers" do what they should do (Wile, 1996)? Successful performance requires that a number of factors be in place, including the skills to perform, personal motivation, the opportunity to perform, coaching and feedback, the right tools, and the belief that one can perform. David Wile synthesized five models that describe why people perform (or don't

Table 3.1
Key Questions for Needs Assessment

The following questions can be used during the performance assessment or training needs assessment process to help uncover key issues about the organization and performance discrepancy at hand.

- What is your vision of this organization? What would it look like if it were successful?
- What are the barriers you think get in the way of this organization's being successful?
- What competition do you have in your market? Has your market recently changed?
- What do customers think of this organization? What would you like customers to think of this organization?
- What do employees think of this organization? What would you like employees to think of this organization?
- What does a successful leader look like to you?
- What do you think managers think of this organization? How would you like managers to think of this organization?
- How does training fit into your strategic plan? How will training help achieve the goals?
- What kind of training have you done in the past?
- Why do you think training will help you with this issue?
- What goals do you have for the training? What problems would you like to solve?
- Who is the training audience? What do they know? What training have they had?
- What support is there for training in the organization? What do employees and managers think of training? What systems are in place to support training?

perform). Experts in the field of human performance—Thomas F. Gilbert, Allison Rossett, Joe Harless, Dean Spitzer, and Robert F. Mager—created the five human performance models. Wile synthesized all of these models into a single framework that describes the various elements that must be present and aligned to ensure that people perform the desired tasks in the right way. These elements are:

- inherent ability
- skills/knowledge
- physical environment
- tools
- cognitive support
- incentives and coaching
- organizational systems

Wile, who included examples of each element in his 1996 work, has used the model to help his clients better understand the set of solutions that may be needed in order to help "doers do." Elements in Wile's model, along with some expanded examples of each, are illustrated in figure 3.1.

THE ASSESSMENT PROCESS

To determine what needs to be done to ensure that performers are doing what they should be doing (that is, to solve a performance problem), train-

Figure 3.1
Human Performance Elements and Examples

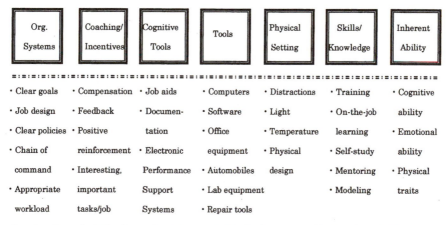

Org. Systems	Coaching/ Incentives	Cognitive Tools	Tools	Physical Setting	Skills/ Knowledge	Inherent Ability
• Clear goals	• Compensation	• Job aids	• Computers	• Distractions	• Training	• Cognitive
• Job design	• Feedback	• Documen-	• Software	• Light	• On-the-job	ability
• Clear policies	• Positive	tation	• Office	• Temperature	learning	• Emotional
• Chain of	reinforcement	• Electronic	equipment	• Physical	• Self-study	ability
command	• Interesting,	Performance	• Automobiles	design	• Mentoring	• Physical
• Appropriate	important	Support	• Lab equipment		• Modeling	traits
workload	tasks/job	Systems	• Repair tools			

Based on: D. Wile, Why doers do (February 1996), *Performance and Instruction*, 30–35.

ing professionals first must analyze the performance problem and identify the root cause. During performance analysis, the analyst should, as Dana and Jim Robinson call it, remain bias-free of solution (Robinson & Robinson, 1995). That is, the training analyst should not be looking for an opportunity to deliver a particular solution, such as providing training. Rather, the analyst should be focused on determining the cause of any performance problems, then determining the appropriate solution or set of solutions to address the performance issue.

Review of Performance Assessment

Mager and Pipe (1984) have described the basic steps for analyzing performance problems. We summarize them here as follows:

I. Describe the performance discrepancy.
   A. Is the discrepancy important?
      1. If no, leave it alone and do nothing.
      2. If yes, begin to determine the cause of the discrepancy, and move to step 2.

II. Determine if there is a skill discrepancy.
   A. If there is a skill discrepancy (that is, the performers do not know how to do something, and they must be able to do it) then:
      1. Determine if the performers have done this task in the past.
         (a) If no, some type of formal training may be needed.
         (b) If yes, determine if the skill is used often.
            (1) If no, practice and/or job aid supports may be needed.
            (2) If yes, feedback may be missing in the system.
      2. Look for the simplest solution, which may include:
         (a) on-the-job training,
         (b) job aids or checklists,
         (c) updated tools, and/or
         (d) changing or refining components of the job.
      3. Determine whether the person or persons have the intellectual capacity to do the job.
         (a) If no, the person is probably wrong for the job.
         (b) If yes, move forward with solutions.
   B. If there is not a skill discrepancy (performers know how to do it but they are not) then:
      1. Determine if the desired performance leads to punishment.
         (a) If this is the case, remove the punishment.
      2. Determine if nonperformance or other performance leads to more favorable consequences.

       (a) If it does, arrange for positive consequences for the desired performance.

   3. Determine if performing the job/task matters to the performers. In other words, is there a meaningful consequence to the desired behavior?

       (a) If not, arrange for a meaningful consequence.

   4. Determine if there are other obstacles preventing performance.

       (a) If there are other obstacles, remove them.

The performance analyst will find that this sequence of steps may change as new information is found. However, to ensure that all necessary solutions have been identified (remember, there is often more than one reason why people are not performing), it is important to go through all of the outlined steps before determining that your analysis is complete (Mager & Pipe, 1984).

Ultimately, the goals of a performance analysis are these:

- to define the desired performance,

- to identify any barriers to or enablers of the desired performance, and

- to determine the set of solutions that needs to be put in place to ensure the desired performance.

The phrase "set of solutions" or "solution system" is often used to describe what needs to be done to solve a performance problem because rarely is lack of performance due to only one factor. Typically, more than one intervention or solution is needed to close a performance gap or to take advantage of a performance improvement opportunity.

Performance assessment must be, as Dana Robinson describes, "like a laser" (D.G. Robinson, personal communication, November 1998). In other words, a performance assessment should be focused, fast, and systematic. The analyst should gather only the most important data that is needed to define the performance, identify barriers and enablers, and determine the set of solutions needed for the performance issue at hand. Depending on the type of assessment, the analyst might choose to talk with two or three exemplars and their supervisors or do a quick survey of a random sample of performers. Some performance assessments take a few days; others may take a few weeks or longer depending on the nature and the scope of the project.

Review of Training Assessment

Now that we've discussed performance assessment, where does training assessment fit in? Well, assume that a performance assessment was conducted and the data have been analyzed. One of the solutions to closing the performance gap might be training. How does the analyst know if training is needed? Following are Mager's (1992) rules for determining if training is needed:

Rule #1: Training is appropriate only when two conditions are present:

a. There is something that one or more persons don't know how to do, and
b. they need to be able to do it.

Rule #2: If they already know how to do something, more training will not help.

When the data show that people don't know how to do something and they need to be able to, then training is appropriate. At that point, a training needs assessment should be conducted. Training needs assessment can be described as a follow-up process that takes performance assessment results and transforms them into the right instruction (Rossett, 1999). During training needs assessment, the training professional must conduct three types of analyses: the audience (learner) analysis, the content analysis, and the organizational analysis (Noe, 1999).

Several sources of information and assessment tools are available to the training analyst in this process. Information sources could be subject matter experts, managers and supervisors, select members of the targeted audience, and the client who has requested the training. Tools and techniques may include focus groups, surveys, individual interviews with subject matter experts (SMEs), and observation. Generally, at least two methods should be used (Noe, 1999). Each type of analysis is discussed in turn.

Audience Analysis. An audience analysis describes the key characteristics of the learners who will participate in the training intervention. Knowing the characteristics of the audience helps training professionals select content, examples, terminology, methodology, program themes, and so on, that will best help participants to understand and absorb the materials. It is important for trainers to thoroughly understand their audience and to tailor the materials to make them as relevant as possible to the participants, so that they have the fewest barriers to learning and internalizing the material. Trainers must find out what the learners already know, what kind of training they have experienced before, and what intellectual level the materials should be geared toward.

For example, at one organization, the training solution involved creating an on-the-job training program that would appeal to a group of cashiers, who were mostly young urban women. It was determined that the materials needed to be as hands-on as possible, fast-paced, and include fun individual challenges that would pique their interest, intellect, and competitive spirit. The wording included terminology from the industry to make it as relevant as possible and to ensure that the participants felt the materials were written specifically for them. Finally, the materials were packaged in a jazzy, stylized format to appeal to the youth and urban sophistication of the group.

Content Analysis. The scope of the training needs to be identified. That is, what should, and should not, be included in the training? There are several types of analysis that training professionals might use to determine the exact content of training. Analysis techniques will vary depending on what skills/tasks performers need to learn. For example, if the training includes step-by-step instructions for completing a new procedure, the training assessment may include conducting a task analysis to describe the step-by step process a performer must go through to complete the job. If the training is to focus on helping performers improve their current performance, it may be optimal to interview or observe exemplars and compare what they are doing and how they are doing it, to what and how more typical performers are doing.

This content analysis should reveal the knowledge and skills that typical performers must possess to do better or differently, in order to improve their performance. This data would produce the core content of the training and would be used to determine the actual learning objectives. Learning objectives describe the outcomes expected from the instruction. They can also be derived (in part) from the performance analysis, as they should reflect what a person should be able to do after the instruction. Finally, during the content assessment, it can also be useful to conduct a skills hierarchy, which shows the order in which skills or knowledge must be learned and sequenced in the instruction.

Organizational Analysis. The third step of training needs assessment—organizational analysis—involves analyzing the organizational factors that may influence the training, including the culture, the general attitude toward training, logistical support for the training, and management support of training. This analysis may also be derived, in part, from the performance assessment but must be analyzed in detail to ensure that the training initiative will have the most support possible within the organization. This analysis is necessary because organizational support is a key factor in ensuring learning transfer. Organizational analysis also helps determine the possible delivery systems for the training intervention, which again ensures the greatest likelihood that the training will actually take place in a way that meets the needs of the trainees and the client.

As a final step in the needs assessment process, all the information is collected in an instructional (or lesson) plan. An instructional plan reflects the results of the analysis and lays out the program goals, objectives, and content outline (Noe, 1999).

Summary of the Assessment Process

Performance assessment and training needs assessment are related but different. Both help training professionals figure out what to do. Performance assessment looks at the larger picture of what level of performance is desired, barriers and enablers to that performance, and what set of solutions can help close performance gaps. If training is one of the solutions necessary to close the performance gap, then a training needs assessment is conducted to analyze the learner, content, and organizational issues that will impact the training.

Is a performance assessment always needed? What about situations where what the doers need to do is something new—something they cannot do now but should be able to do? Then, training is definitely needed. Is a performance assessment needed in this case? Yes, because of Mager's (1992) following rule:

Rule #3: Skill alone is not enough to guarantee performance.

Remember, numerous elements impact why doers do! Furthermore, there are times when a client asks for training, and a change in performance is not the goal. The trainer finds this out by asking the client questions about desired outcomes of the training or about what people need to be able to do better or differently as a result of the training (what the performance goal is). If there is not a performance goal—say for example, the client's goal is to make people aware of a new idea—a performance assessment would not be needed. This would be a request for information or education and the training professional would conduct an analysis to determine what the content of the educational intervention needs to be.

CASE EXAMPLES—INTERNAL CONSULTING

The case examples in this section are based, in part, on the real-life experiences of various in-house training personnel. Each of the three cases illustrates the initial expectations of internal client groups and how the different internal clients reacted to questions and suggestions from the training representative. The reader should note how the training professional in these examples (identified as Jose) shows flexibility in responding to client requests and in flexing his professional abilities to meet client needs.

Scenario 1: Responding to a Request for Training

(*Phone rings*) Hello, this is the training department, Jose speaking.

Client: Hi Jose, this is Claudette Noir. I am the new director in the global marketing group. Bob Smith recommended I call you. He said you would know some really great team-building activities. I am meeting with my team at the end of next week, and I would like for you to come to our meeting and lead a two-hour team-building training session. We meet at 8:00 on Monday. Can you make it?

In this request, the client has already identified a need and has determined a training solution (team-building training) and has even determined the amount of time it should take! Jose has a choice to make here. He can commit to doing this team-building training as re-

quested, and ask more questions about the logistics of the event, or he can ask questions to determine if there is a performance need (that is, do a performance assessment).

Jose: Hi, Claudette. Bob told me you might be calling. He said you had been in your present job for about two months and might call to find out about some of our products and services. So, you are meeting with your team next week and you would like some team-building training. Please tell me a little bit about what you want your team to be doing more, better, or differently as a result of having gone through team-building training.

Jose does not commit to delivering training as a solution to the client's perceived performance problem. Rather, he asks a question to better understand the level and type of performance Claudette wants from her team.

Claudette: Well, frankly, I want them to stop arguing over resources. Our last team two meetings did not go well. Almost everyone was angry by the end of the meetings, and we still hadn't decided how to resource one of our biggest projects. We're losing time and I'm losing my patience. If they can't work as a team and come to agreements on resourcing issues, I'm going to make the decisions myself. I'd prefer we worked together and come to agreements as a team on these issues. I want some training to help us out.

Jose: What do you think is going on with your team? What is preventing them from making decisions about resources?

Jose is asking for Claudette's opinion. He has not yet offered any solutions or committed to deliver training. He is asking questions.

Claudette: Right before I took over as director, this department had a budget cut. The department had to take 15 percent out of the budget, and the previous director reassigned two associates to different projects without asking anyone. Almost everyone in the department is angry and a little nervous wondering if there will be more cuts and reassignments. I was thinking that if we had some training on how to work together under stress it would help.

Jose: So your team is feeling stressed and they aren't sharing resources. You want them to work together to make resource decisions. To help me understand a little more about the situation, can you tell me if there has been a time when your team has worked well together—when they worked in a way that you would like for them to work all of the time?

Claudette: Well, let's see. They did a great job of helping me to create a presentation for our executive committee the second week I was here. I was new and needed their help in preparing a report of the team's accomplishments so far this year. We had a great meeting where we built the outline of the presentation together, and then everyone pitched in, gathered data, and shared information. Some of them stayed late to help each other and to help me finish parts of the presentation. It was great. I want them to work that way all of the time.

Jose: So you have seen them cooperate and share work together, and in fact, they have done it in a way that was very productive.

Claudette: Yes. What is your point?

Jose: Well, when people are not doing what you want them to do, one reason might be because they don't know how. If they don't know how, then training can help them learn how. It sounds like your team knows how to make some decisions, then cooperate and share. They just aren't doing it in these types of situations.

Jose is summarizing what he has heard. He also provides Claudette with some information to help her understand that training might not be the answer.

Claudette: What do you suggest then?

Jose: I would like to help you with this. It would be helpful to know more about why they aren't sharing resources, cooperating, and making decisions together in this situation. Then we could remove those barriers. Would it be okay if I talked to a few of your team members to find out more about the situation from their viewpoint? Then I would be better able to help you find a way to work through this.

Jose reinforces that he wants to help Claudette. He asks for permission to find out more about the situation, in other words, to conduct a quick assessment. Note that Jose does not use the word "assessment." Jose has not yet determined a solution but has agreed to help the client figure it out.

Claudette: I guess so. I don't want this to take a lot of time, but it might be helpful to know more. I just haven't had the time to talk with them one-to-one about this. I still want you to come to our staff meeting next week, and I want you to help us work through this. We've spent way too much time on this already.

Jose: Great. Since you have eight direct reports, I would probably be able to meet with most of them in the next few days. I would only need about forty-five minutes with each. After that, you and I can look at what they are saying and determine what the right actions might be to take. Would that be okay with you?

Jose is reviewing his plan with Claudette and including her in the review of data and decision-making. They will look at the data together and determine actions together, in partnership. He also asks for her approval and commitment to his plan.

Claudette: That sounds reasonable to me. I'll send you our organization chart so you know who is on my team.

Jose: Okay. It would be great if you would leave a short voicemail for your team and let them know I'll be scheduling some time to talk with them to help the team work together better on the budget issues. Would you be willing to do this today?

Jose makes sure to have Claudette tell her direct reports that she has asked him to work with them. Since Claudette is the sponsor of this project, it is her role to position this with her team. Jose also asks for Claudette to take immediate action—call her team today.

Summary Points. While this situation may not require a major, corporate-wide needs analysis to help the company take advantage of a unique business opportunity, it is representative of some of the requests that training personnel receive. These situations provide training professional opportunities to develop skills in looking across the entire system of a small group or department to determine what set of solutions need to be in place in order to achieve the desired type and level of performance.

When Jose talks to the team members, he may find any number of things in the system that need to be addressed. For example, the team may not want to make the decision. The team may believe Claudette should make the final decision as their previous director did (even though they complained about that approach and did not like the decision). The team may not have all of the data they need to make the decision. Part of the issue may be that they do not know which projects are most important to accomplishing the department's goals. In addition, Claudette may not be clear about her expectations. Or they may not have a clear process for making decisions. Ultimately, it is likely that there is more than one barrier getting in the way of this team performing the way that Claudette prefers. And Jose has turned a request for training—where training was not likely to help or to be the only solution—into an opportunity to work with the team to find the solution, or set of solutions, that will help this group solve a business problem.

At this point, Jose will now turn his attention to conducting his data collection by preparing questions that will help him gather the appropriate data during his interviews with the team members. He will want to have a consistent approach and set of questions for each interview. It is critical that Jose has developed the ability to ask questions in a logical sequence and with appropriate probing when the answers don't provide specific information. After the data collection, Jose will categorize and analyze the information he has received and will formulate some opinions about the data and some preliminary recommendations. When he meets with Claudette to review the data, he will ask for her opinions, share his, and together they will determine what steps to take. It may be that they decide to share the data with the entire team and have the team help determine what actions to take. Let's consider another scenario.

Scenario 2: Responding to a Request for Education

(*Knocking*) Hi Jose, I'm Stefan Weber. We have an appointment to talk about some training for the administrative assistant conference.

Jose: Yes, come on in. I remember from your e-mail that you are one of the administrative assistants responsible for organizing this year's admin conference. How can I help you?

Stefan: Well, I know that this training department offers a one-day training session to help people understand the corporate strategy. We would like for you or someone from your department to come to the admin conference and deliver a two-hour version of this for us. We'd really appreciate it. We are having two other workshops, one on career development for administrative assistants and one on the new e-mail system.

Here again, Jose has a choice to make. He can agree to deliver the training, or he can find out more about the situation, more about what performance improvements the administrative assistants might want or need to make.

Jose: I see. Can you tell me a little bit more about how you choose topics for the conference? It would help me better understand the situation.

Stefan: Well, this is an annual conference planned by administrative assistants for administrative assistants. Every year we do a survey of the assistants to find out what they most want to learn about. This year, the corporate strategy was one of the most requested topics.

Jose: Can you tell me a little more about why this topic was requested?

Stefan: That's a good question. I wondered about that too, so I did a little research. It turns out that in the last two years we have had a lot of experienced administrative assistants retire, so we hired new people to replace them. In addition, the number of assistants has increased recently to help support the expansion of the sales force, so we have a lot of new assistants in the company who are curious about the company's strategy for growth. In our jobs, we aren't always invited to meetings where this is discussed. We have heard about all of the new products being developed and how our business is expanding around the world. We are interested in learning more about the company.

Stefan has already gathered some data about the situation. Jose will follow up with a specific question about performance.

Jose: That is great. It sounds like your group wants more information. Tell me, after this workshop is over, what would the assistants like to be able to do better?

Stefan: Well, we really just want to understand more about the strategy, vision, and mission. We aren't involved in creating or developing strategy really. We just think this information will give us a better understanding of the company overall, and help us better understand some of the projects we help out with.

From Stefan's description, Jose believes an educational session, to create greater awareness of the strategy and build knowledge seems appropriate. Jose might work with Stefan to identify learning objectives for the session and begin to design the session. Or, Jose might help Stefan find someone else in the department who specializes in designing and developing educational sessions who can help meet Stefan's need.

Summary Points. Not every request for training will or should lead to a formal in-depth needs assessment. There are times when educational sessions are needed and should be provided in a quality, customer-focused way. Basic knowledge is needed for people to do their jobs, understand the context in which they work, and ensure that they feel a part of the team or organization. On the other hand, it will still be important for the training department to ask questions in all three needs assessment categories—what is the profile of the learner, what does the learner already know, and what is the best way to deliver this material to them? Also, what exact content should be covered and what is the best way to deliver this material in the two-hour session?

In this situation, Jose asked questions to determine if the client was seeking a specific change in performance. The answer was "no"—so a pure awareness-raising session seems appropriate in this setting. It is important that Jose explored this situation and is clear on the expectations and needs.

Scenario 3: Proactively Identifying Performance Needs

Jose has been aware of a major reengineering project taking place in the human resources (HR) group for the last six months. Many of the HR processes have been reengineered to help simplify how work gets done and to increase the efficiency and effectiveness of the services that HR provides to the organization. In addition to reengineering processes, the project team has also recommended that the HR generalist job focus on two main roles, one dedicated to organization effectiveness and the other dedicated to employee relations (working directly with employees to help them with their development planning and any employee issues that might arise). Not much work was done to describe these roles, just a few paragraphs outlining some of the key reasons for the roles and a general description of what people in these roles might do.

Recently, Jose was asked to participate in a meeting where the two new roles were to be discussed and given further definition and clarity. Jose was asked to listen to the discussion so that he could begin to make some recommendations for what types of training might be needed. The participants at the meeting were members of the reengineering team and current HR generalists from within the organization and around the world. As Jose listened, the discussion quickly turned into more of a debate and complaint session about what the roles should really be. The conversation went something like this:

HR manager 1: What exactly do you mean by organization effectiveness? Does that mean we want HR generalists to focus on reengineering work? My customers won't go for that.

Project leader: No, that's not what it means. It means helping your internal customers diagnose organizational problems and finding the root causes. Then your customers can determine what to do to address the issues.

Personnel rep: Oh, man. I am already swamped with personnel issues and just running our day-to-day HR tools and processes. I don't have time to do organizational diagnosis.

HR manager 2: That's true. My team members are already working ten- and twelve-hour days. We can't add one more thing to their plates.

Project leader: Well, we'd have to stop doing some of the other things we do today and reprioritize the work.

HR manager 3: Organizational diagnosis? How are we supposed to learn more about this? My team is good, but we haven't done this type of work in a long time.

HR manager 2: Isn't that what the organization effectiveness department is supposed to do? If we start doing this, what will they do?

HR manager 1: Will somebody read the descriptions of the roles again? How is the organization effectiveness role different from the employee relations role? Would we have one person doing both or would it require two people? I can't add any people to my department.

HR manager 4: This is very much what we are doing in Europe today. I don't see how this changes anything for those of us working in Europe.

HR manager 3: (To project leader) What exactly did the reengineering team think people would be doing in these new roles?

Project leader: That's what we want you to help us figure out.

Summary Points. Not much was accomplished in this meeting. Almost everyone in the room agreed with the general statements about the new roles. However, everyone had a different idea about exactly what an HR generalist would be doing when these new roles were implemented. In addition, several people mentioned significant barriers to accomplishing the things they thought necessary to perform these roles (time constraints, customer preferences, lack of ability, and so on). From these discussions, Jose realizes that there was not enough clarity about the roles to even begin to think about how to support the transition to these new roles, let alone to conduct a training needs analysis to determine the type of education and training that might be needed to support these new roles.

Jose knows that this HR reengineering project is significantly changing the way that HR does business and interacts with customers. The results of this project will have a major impact on the entire organization. While Jose was invited into this project to help determine what training might be needed, he sees the need for performance analysis first. This is the type of large-scale performance project that is likely to have high visibility in the organization, require sponsorship from an executive, require collecting data from multiple sources, and result in a set of solutions designed to change the system in which these new roles will need to operate. Training is likely to be only one component of the solution.

After discussing this with his colleagues, Jose believes that creating a "performance model" for each of these new roles would be the best place to start this performance work. In a performance model, the *results* that each role will be required to deliver will be defined, as well as, the *best practices* for how to accomplish those results. In addition, the *measures* of success will be identified, as well as the *barriers* and *enablers* to achieving the results. A performance model will help clear up the confusion that exists about the roles and will provide data to help determine what actions to take to support the new roles.

Jose knows the person responsible for defining the roles and for implementing the roles globally; her name is Marilyn. Marilyn is an experienced, highly skilled HR professional who has never been responsible for implementing a project of this magnitude. Jose knows she is looking for a way to define the roles and implement them globally. He decides that he will proactively set up some time to talk with Marilyn about a way that he can help her define the roles and find out what needs to be done to implement them. He will show her a sample from a performance model and find out if that would meet her needs. If Marilyn likes what she sees in the model, they will talk about what it would take to create the model and move forward from there.

In this particular case, the internal client, Marilyn, agreed that the performance model would help solve her problem, and Jose and Marilyn co-led the analysis that ended in the creation of two performance models (one for each of the new HR generalist roles). They also worked with the project steering team to determine the set of solutions that needed to be in place to implement the new roles. While Jose was responding to a request from a client (that is, sit in on this meeting and help us determine what training needs to be created), he identified the need to conduct a needs analysis, to create performance models, and to identify the set of solutions required for supporting performance in the workplace. This was truly an opportunity for large-scale performance work that Jose was able to co-lead because of his proactive approach and ability to see beyond one solution (training) in the overall picture of employee performance.

Challenges in Internal Needs Assessment

Contrary to Jose's approach in the preceding examples, many companies and their internal training personnel have taken a mostly traditional approach to training needs assessment. This traditional approach has included training professionals working as "pairs-of-hands" (Block, 1981), with the internal client determining the problem and solution and the training representative creating training materials without being in a true partnership. In other words, the established approach has been characterized by situations with optional front-end assessments; where training is viewed as an end in itself, a check-the-box exercise, or a fun event; and finally, where Level 1 (reaction) and Level 2 (learning) evaluations are generally the only levels of evaluation used (Robinson & Robinson, 1995). In these environments, training groups can spend up to 80 to 90 percent of their time responding to client requests and about 10 to 20 percent of their time proactively identifying performance issues and working with clients to close performance gaps in a systemic way.

However, as illustrated in the preceding examples, other training professionals have begun to stretch the boundaries of the traditional needs assessment approach by invoking a more performance-based approach. In other words, they use performance-focused questions and assessments with their client groups more often. To be expected, not every internal client group is comfortable with this approach, and some clients find it odd that training personnel would ask about "what the performers should be able to do," and odder still that a training representative would want to know what business goals need to be achieved. At the same time, these clients end up being much happier with the ultimate solutions they receive.

Having said that, this more contemporary needs assessment approach is not without other challenges. Some training professionals are uncomfortable with the transition to the performance-based needs analysis approach. Many want to use their talents and skills primarily to design, develop, and deliver excellent training solutions when they are needed. These skills in design, development, and delivery of training are highly valued and will remain so. However, the additional use of performance assessments, which look at the entire system in which performance takes place, will help to ensure that when training *is* one of the solutions that is needed, what is learned will be supported and reinforced in the work environment, making the return on investment on training even greater.

Using the aforementioned performance assessment model will help today's training professionals avoid their bias toward training solutions that may fail to help. On the other hand, when training is the obvious need, a structured training analysis that covers all three bases (learner, content, and organization) will ensure the best possible intervention.

CASE EXAMPLES—EXTERNAL CONSULTING

The following cases are based, in part, on the real-life experiences of various external training consultants who have been asked to assess and implement training solutions in numerous organizations. Each of the cases illustrates the initial expectations of external client groups and how the different clients reacted to questions and suggestions from the external training consultant. The reader should note how the training professional in these examples conducted a needs analysis that determined, in the first case, that training *was not* the appropriate first solution, and in the second, that training *was* the appropriate solution.

Scenario A: Responding to a Request for Training

The company in this situation is an established firm that had recently merged with another company. The newly merged company was attempting a major revitalization of the business, including developing a new image and identity, conducting a new marketing campaign, and undertaking a major remodeling initiative. The organization's management thought the firm might need training for existing employees to help them perform better in the revitalized company, in which customer expectations would be higher. Sales training and customer service training seemed like obvious choices. But before committing to a particular training solution, the training consultants requested permission to conduct a broad-based organizational performance assessment to determine what the issues were and what solutions (training or not) might be appropriate.

Assessment Process. The consultants first interviewed the two key managers for the newly merged company to determine what their goals for the organization were, what they considered to be the key performance issues, and what their training goals might be. The training manager for the organization, who was relatively new to his position and the training profession, was also interviewed so that the external consultants could establish a positive relationship and work closely with the training department.

Meetings were held with the graphic design firm, the marketing firm, and the interior design firm, to determine what issues they had identified and how performance improvement and training interventions could be aligned with their improvement efforts to better help the client. The training consultants also toured the work site and observed customer interactions to determine the quality of the sales and service experience.

Focus groups were set up with employees to find out what customer issues they faced, what internal obstacles they had, and what skills they felt they lacked in order to perform effectively in their jobs. A two-page survey was distributed, with the following questions:

1. What do you enjoy most about your job? What gives you the most satisfaction? What do you take pride in the most?
2. What are the greatest obstacles that get in the way of you performing at your highest levels? (internally or externally)
3. When one of your customers is angry or upset, what do they say? (Use exact words.)
4. When one of your customers is confused, what do they say? (Use exact words.)
5. When one of your customers is delighted, what do they say? (Use exact words.)
6. If you could get training in any one area, what would it be? Why?
7. If you could do one thing to improve your job or the service you provide to your customers, what would it be?

At the focus groups, employees filled out the questionnaires silently, then had the opportunity to discuss each question as a group. At the initial focus groups, it was immediately apparent that the organization was facing major problems that were beyond the scope of a training solution. Employees were disgruntled, angry, upset, and clearly not aligned with management. Issues left over from the merger were clearly not resolved as the merger was perceived as an invasion of the old company, especially since management from the new company was now in charge. The organization's performance seemed to be seriously hampered by these internal issues and resistance to change. Sales were down, refunds were up, and employee enthusiasm and motivation were seriously challenged. Employees were not working together within their teams or within the larger company.

After the initial focus groups, the external consultants decided to interview all the key managers involved, starting with the CEO, to determine what their vision for the organization was and to determine what obstacles they felt were in the way. Each manager was probed in depth about the issues and challenges he/she faced. The two key managers of the division were reinterviewed, and the performance and organizational issues were more deeply probed.

All the information from the interviews, focus groups, site tours, and product assessments were collected into an in-depth report and presented to the top management team. As a result of this comprehensive needs assessment process, the consultants were able to demonstrate in their report that while training might be part of the solution for this company, the organization was not yet ready for it. The opinion of the consultants was that due to the major issues faced by the organization, a *comprehensive organizational development* process was needed. The consultants provided a list of characteristics of companies that are ripe for an organizational transformation effort, and showed how the division met almost all of the criteria, including these:

- The organization was undergoing transition from one stage of growth to another.

- The organization lacked direction due to an inappropriate organizational structure.

- There was a sense of unrealized potential for the company.

- The organization was in an "identity crisis," lacking a clear sense of purpose or direction.

- The organization was clinging to obsolete products, services, or practices.

- The organization was experiencing low staff morale and high turnover.

- The organization had grown very quickly, past the "Mom and Pop" stage.

- There was conflict about the organization's direction.

- The organization had experienced major changes in its environment, for example, a merger and office rearrangements.

- The organization had implemented new technology.

- The organization was bogged down with inflexible rules and directives.

- There were people in place who were stopping or hindering progress.

- The organization's external environment (market, etc.) had changed dramatically by becoming more competitive.

- Decision-making was slow, communication was ineffective, and creativity was lacking.

As a result of the needs assessment process, the consultants recommended a number of interventions, including a strategic planning session by the top management. Once the planning was done to determine top priorities, the consultants recommended a process improvement initiative, beginning with a management retreat, and followed by weekly meetings and educational sessions with the management team. Another consultant specializing in process improvement was brought on to the consulting team to help facilitate the process. The goal was to help the team begin to work together more closely to identify and analyze problems, get ownership of the problems, and learn to use the tools and techniques that would help more consistently meet their customer and employee expectations. The process improvement initiative would also uncover training needs and allow the management team to prioritize them and provide training on an as-needed basis. Additionally, an executive coach was hired to work with the CEO, who was relatively new to the industry and the company, to provide support and help manage his relationship with other key managers.

Summary Points. This project started out with a training focus, but by keeping an open mind about possible solutions and conducting a thorough needs assessment the consultants and the client were able to react appropriately when the depth of the performance problems and employees issues was discovered. The managers had been moving so quickly, without real knowledge of how to orchestrate change effectively in an organization, that they didn't realize what a negative impact they were having on employees and customers. They needed someone they could trust to help guide them through a self-discovery process and to implement appropriate solutions.

This example shows how a training consultant needs to be able to partner with the organization to uncover issues, to remain open to whether or not training is a solution, and to recommend nontraining solutions when appropriate. This requires knowledge of other forms of interventions (for example, organizational development), and knowledge of other resources that are available to lead the alternate intervention (for example, process improvement coaching, executive coaching). This example also shows how it can be important for the training consultant to educate the client about the options available, other than pure training, to solve performance issues.

Scenario B: Responding to Another Request for Training

The organization in this situation is a large national franchise organization that needed to develop a training program for front-line employees on how to function effectively as a service provider for the organization. Retail sales are the focus of this company, and employees did not have any consistent, effective method for learning to perform the tasks involved. The group met with a training consulting firm to determine how to go about the process of developing the training program. At the first meeting, the conversation went something like this:

Consultant: Tell me what's wrong with the current way you're training people. What seems to be the problem?

Client: Well, first of all, we don't really even have a training method. People can literally just get hired and start working. They might let the person work with someone else the first day, if that person's not too busy. But we can't say for sure if that person even really knows what they're doing. Even if it's the manager, he/she is usually too busy to be very effective. They don't know how to train someone in the first place!

Consultant: Tell me about the employees. What are they like?

Client: Well, most new employees are pretty young—high school or college age. They want to work part-time, and their hours need to be flexible since they're usually in school. They like our stores because they're pretty hip and clean and healthy—it's a good job. But with our current training, they usually feel awkward in the beginning—like they don't belong. So lots of times they'll just quit. They get frustrated and don't want to stay. They hate to look like idiots when a customer asks them for something and they don't know what to say. So, we have a lot of turnover in our new hires.

It is obvious from the initial questions that no training systems are in place and that more formal systems are needed. Trainees cannot perform effectively even if they want to. An initial assessment of the performance gap shows that performance is hampered by lack of systems, not lack of motivation. The initial questioning also helps analyze the learner, helping to clarify what the targeted audience is like.

Client: Well, first of all, we want our new hires to like working here, and take pride in their work. I mean, it's a good brand and a good product, and they should feel good about it. We want them to stick around, especially after we've trained them! And we want them all to get trained more quickly and effectively, but somewhat independently, since sometimes we'll be so busy we won't be able to have someone working with them. Plus, we want everyone to be trained the same way so that they are consistent in the way they service our customers. And of course we want them to be able to deliver great service, so our customers will continue to want to come back. We have to be able to present a strong brand to our customers to represent good service.

The training system may have to be learner-directed so the new employee has a way of managing his/her training even if a trainer is not available. Self-paced training manuals may be helpful so employees can learn independently from their trainer if need be. This may help to avoid the feeling of awkwardness for the new, young employee.

Consultant: Okay, so tell me more about what it's like when new employees get hired. What happens to them?

Client: Well, we usually just go over the employee rules with them and introduce them to everyone, if we can. Then we let them start behind the counter. Like I said, we have them work with someone if we can, but pretty much, it's sink or swim.

The logistics of the system will have to be managed carefully as there will be little organizational support for training, especially if it is labor intensive for the manager or other employees.

Consultant: Okay, so what kinds of things do you want these employees to know? What should they get training in?

Client: Well, they need to know how to make our product and how to take a cus-tomer order. They need to run the cash register. And they need to be able to stock up behind the counter so they don't get slammed when it's busy. And they need to know something about our other retail products in the store so they can help cus-tomers if they ask them about an item.

The basic learning objectives of the training have been identified.

Consultant: Do they take a tour of the store when they start?

Client: Well, not really. I mean, sort of. But sometimes we need somebody immedi-ately when they get hired, so we just put them to work!

Consultant: If we did develop an employee training system, how do we know it will be used? Sounds like employees just get put to work and that managers might not even use the training if we gave it to them.

Client: Yeah, that's a problem. After all, these are franchise owners, and we can't force them to use the training. So we've got to sell the idea to them.

Consultant: What support do you have for this from the top management?

Client: Good support. I mean, they're all for it, but they want us to tell them how it should be done.

Getting the top management to agree to the importance of the training, even in a fran-chise operation, will be essential to selling the idea to franchisees.

Consultant: OK, let's summarize what we've talked about so far. You need a training system that will appeal to your training audience, which is a young, hip, Generation X-type group. It needs to help these trainees feel less awkward in those first few days, so they're more likely to stick around and feel a sense of belonging and pride. It needs to be service focused and consistent across all stores to effectively promote your brand. It needs to be something that's learner-directed, something that the trainee can use whether or not there's a trainer available. And it needs to show the trainee all the basics of working the counter, plus the retail side, and the inventory and stocking side.

Client: Yes, that's it! Can we do all that?

Consultant: I think so, but we need to figure out a plan to help us get there and a way to gather organizational support.

Client: Well, we want to introduce this at our franchisee-owner meeting in a couple of months, so we could use that as a time to introduce this to them and get them to see the benefit of it. Do we have enough time to get this together by then?

Consultant: Well, let's look at a timeline and see what we need to do . . .

Summary Points. This case, which starts out as a performance assess-ment, clearly calls for a training solution. Since no training systems or methods are currently in place, the trainees could not be effective even if they wanted to be (remember Mager's test). And it is clear that the trainees do want to be effective but are frustrated in their efforts. So it was appropri-ate to quickly move into a training needs assessment in the initial meeting. The learner analysis, organizational analysis, and content analysis have already indicated the basic needs that can and will be addressed through training.

CONCLUSION

Performance assessment is the first step of assessing any stated training need. The question is, given the existing performance and the desired performance, is training a possible solution? If not, what other solutions should be implemented? And if so, what are the learner, organizational, and content needs to be addressed by the training? A thorough assessment during the performance analysis, and a thorough assessment during the training needs analysis, will provide the necessary direction for implementing a solution. Ultimately, however, training professionals must be open to considering all the options based upon the situation before them, and should not jump to a training solution when it is not appropriate.

BIBLIOGRAPHY

Block, P. (1981). *Flawless consulting: A guide to getting your expertise used.* Austin, TX: Learning Concepts.

Mager, R.F. (1992). *What every manager should know about training or "I've got a training problem"* . . . *and other odd ideas.* Belmont, CA: Lake Publishing Company.

Mager, R.F., & Pipe, P. (1984). *Analyzing performance problems or you really oughta wanna.* (2nd ed). Belmont, CA: Lake Publishing Company.

Noe, R.A. (1999). *Employee training & development.* Boston, MA: Irwin McGraw-Hill.

Robinson, D.G., & Robinson, J. (1995). *Performance consulting: Moving beyond training.* San Francisco: Berett-Koehler Publishers.

Rossett, A. (1987). *Training needs assessment.* Englewood Cliffs, NJ: Educational Technology Publications.

Rossett, A. (1999). *First things fast: A handbook for performance analysis.* San Francisco: Jossey-Bass Pfeiffer.

Wile, D. (1996). Why doers do. *Performance and Instruction, 35,* 30–35.

Chapter 4

Technological Advancements in Training Design, Delivery, Support, and Administration

Larry A. Pace

Consider the following: Dwaine Pope, a Texas-based management consultant, sits at a desk in Stamford, Connecticut, participating in a company-sponsored program on his laptop computer. Pope is on a work assignment but has set aside time for the scheduled course. He dials in to the company server, enters his password, and is logged on to the training session. The company instructors in Philadelphia interact with Pope and up to 249 other remote learners by using a program called Centra 99. Learners see the presentation slides and hear the instructors through their computer speakers (or through earphones).

When Pope needs clarification, he clicks on a hand-shaped icon to indicate his desire to ask a question. His username is placed in the queue with those of other participants, whose queries are addressed in turn. When the instructor recognizes a questioner, he or she speaks into the microphone to pose the question. Learners hear both the questions asked by other students and the answers given by the instructors. Periodically, the software presents questions that each participant answers to determine whether he or she is learning the course materials. The computer keeps track of participation, sign-on and sign-off times, and student performance on the quizzes.

Students register themselves for courses, and only registered students may participate in a session. Although this system is not fully visually interactive, it does capture much of the essence of a classroom setting. Pope's company, consulting powerhouse PriceWaterhouseCoopers (PWC), with approximately 140,000 employees worldwide, delivers approximately half of its company-sponsored training via distance learning.

Mr. Pope is no stranger to distance learning, having completed many of his MBA course requirements online. His assessment of the PWC courses taught via Centra 99 is that they are every bit as engaging and educational as classroom-based courses. He believes the key to the success of this program is the accountability built into the system. He knows that if he does not participate, does not answer questions, or answers the questions incorrectly, these facts will be recorded. While being empowered, Pope is simultaneously being held accountable.

BACKGROUND

Just as technology plays a significant role today in the company-sponsored learning of Dwaine Pope, from the beginning of history new technologies have influenced training and learning. At first, technology was the subject of training; recently, technology has played an even more significant role, for example, as a source of new training delivery methods.

Soon after every new technique or technology was discovered or invented, someone was showing another person how to use it. Initially, this knowledge was passed from generation to generation by demonstration and the spoken word. Later, written records and then the printed word were used to document and standardize instructional materials. However, the process of training itself remained primarily a stand-and-deliver activity. Learning and technology developed hand in hand. The invention of the printing press sparked a revolution in the distribution of information and the ability to provide training materials to people in geographically dispersed locations. More recently, the computer and the World Wide Web have created an even more revolutionary possibility—that of any computer connected to the Internet as a potential student desk in a worldwide classroom. During a lull in activity between scheduled flights, an employee of U.S. Airways takes a ten-minute quiz on customer service techniques by using one of the many computer terminals at her home airport. Not only does the computer instruct her, but it also scores her performance and records that performance as part of her records.

Today, technology and training are merging as "embedded" features of the school and work performance environment. In the past, the focus was often on the technology itself—the learning of the technology was as daunting a task as learning the subject matter (if not more so). For example, a learner in a word processing course first had to learn to operate the computer that ran the word processing program. The future holds the promise of "invisible" technology that provides a readily available combination of learning and productivity enhancement whenever needed by the knowledge worker.

As technology is embedded and immediately available, it ceases to be the focus of attention. As a case in point, consider computer technologies. While the personal computer is still a separate and useful product, more and more products and services are incorporating computer-processing power in a way that is largely transparent to the user. Microprocessors improve the functionality and features of automobiles, copying machines, electronic devices, and even microwave ovens and other kitchen appliances. One hardly even thinks of the computer technology used in scanning items purchased at a grocery store, but inventory levels, prices, reorder points, and cash flow are all implemented, monitored, linked, and controlled via computer. Many readers, however, will remember the not-too-distant past in which a checkout clerk literally keyed in the price of each item into a cash register, and inventory control was a manual process.

THE ROLE OF TECHNOLOGY IN TRAINING

Technology has a significant impact on the design, development, delivery, support, and administration of training programs. New technologies involving the Internet, company Intranets, multimedia, computer-assisted training, interactive video, virtual reality, and distance learning have brought the Information Revolution, knowledge workers, and the training profession face to face. Some training professionals have resisted or resented the incursion of technology into the domain of training, while others have embraced technology, recognizing the potential benefits of using technology to enhance, to extend, or in some cases to replace traditional training methods.

For centuries, the "technology" for delivering training materials changed very little. Chalkboards and classrooms coupled with captive learners dominated the educational landscape. Incremental improvements included overhead projectors, training films, tapes, and videos, but the model of classroom teaching and learning was unchanged.

The computer, however, offered an alternative delivery mechanism. At the end of the twentieth century, the American Society for Training and Development (ASTD) predicted that advances in computer technology would revolutionize training delivery. Developments in hardware, computer networking, multimedia software, and videoconferencing have tremendous potential for multiple-site delivery and for bringing training closer to people's work sites (ASTD, 1997). ASTD further noted that technology holds the promise of the following improvements:

- *Greater cost-effectiveness.* More people can be trained more often, at a reduced cost, and with increased flexibility to add participants without additional cost.

- *Increased quality of instruction.* Access is available to remote experts, and there are more program choices, as well as multiple opportunities for instructor and participant interaction.

- *Self-paced, individualized instruction.* Participants can learn at levels comfortable for them, at times convenient to them.

- *Fewer resource requirements.* Classrooms, trainers, and other classroom-related resources are not needed.

- *Decentralized training.* Learning can occur anytime, anywhere, and anyplace.

- *Tireless delivery.* Trainers can get tired, but technology is always available for consistent delivery.

Surveys indicate that instructor-led corporate training programs and other classes using the traditional lecture approach are still alive and well, and will perhaps never be fully replaced by technology. However, the growth in the use of new training technologies is impressive. Knowledge workers in the information economy will be compensated as much for their learning as for their performance. E-learning is a growing business. In fact, separating e-learning from e-commerce may be a difference without a distinction since many companies are cashing in on the opportunity to provide learning for profit.

In addition to training delivery, technological advancements are affecting the design of training programs, training support, and the managers and administrators of training programs. The role of technology in training falls into several overlapping categories as shown in figure 4.1. Each of these areas will be discussed in turn.

TRAINING DELIVERY TECHNOLOGIES

Knowledge workers like Dwaine Pope are receiving more and more company-sponsored training via computer. Pope is not alone. For example, Blackboard, an online learning company, provides e-learning software that is used by more than three thousand companies, colleges, schools, and associations in all fifty states of the United States and seventy other countries. Blackboard allows instructors to offer online courses, learners to take classes and conduct online research, and institutions to use the Internet for enhancing both teaching and learning. The use of newly invented technologies to enhance the delivery of training content, however, is not at all new. The introduction of the teaching machine predates the computer by many years.

Teaching Machines

In 1924 Sidney Pressey invented a machine that provided the learner immediate feedback as to whether or not the answer to a multiple-choice

Figure 4.1
The Role of Technology in Training

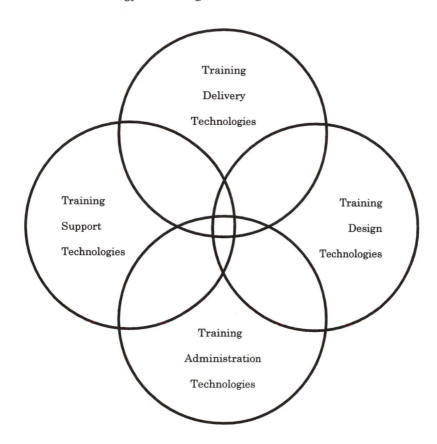

question was correct. If the answer was incorrect, the "auto-instructional" device would not permit the next question to appear until the learner selected the correct answer.

Pressey applied Thorndike's Law of Effect, which states that behavior is a function of its consequences (Brown & Hernstein, 1975). The teaching machine provided positive feedback in the form of a buzzer or a light whenever a correct answer was selected (Pressey, 1950). Though some educators saw Pressey's machine as nothing more than a testing device, Pressey himself saw the opportunity to use the machine for instructional purposes. By ensuring that the device would not advance to the next frame until the correct answer was selected, and by reinforcing correct answers, Pressey had created a simple programmed instruction machine.

The teaching machine did not catch on during the 1920s and the period of the Great Depression. Educators and the public were not ready for an "industrial revolution" in the schoolroom. But after World War II, renewed interest in such devices was sparked when B. F. Skinner (1954) applied his theory of operant conditioning to the educational process. Teaching machines were the precursors both of simulators and computer-based training (CBT) models.

Simulators

Training simulators followed the teaching machine. Simulators are in wide use today. They range from highly sophisticated and expensive flight simulators to fairly simple devices that help physicians in training to learn to sew sutures correctly. Simulators seek to reproduce the psychological and behavioral requirements of a job situation, often in addition to providing some degree of resemblance to the physical work environment. Simulator devices may or may not have fidelity to the actual performance environment, but to be effective, they must have a high degree of psychological fidelity. The behavioral and motor skills employed must have a strong connection to the target behaviors required on the job to facilitate positive transfer.

Flight simulators have saved millions of dollars in equipment costs and have avoided untold human tragedy as pilots have learned in a simulator to react to and deal effectively with conditions such as wind shear. Before simulators could allow the creation of such conditions in a controlled environment, pilots often received only one opportunity to learn to survive wind shear. Sadly, many pilots failed this test. In the simulator, one can learn from experience, make adjustments, and get a second chance. In real life, the pilot only gets one chance. Simulators have been described as useful for the three reasons described below (see Goldstein, 1993).

Replication of the performance environment. Simulators provide the opportunity to reproduce the learning environment under the control of the trainer. Simulators allow the creation of learning conditions that can compress, repeat, or expand the time allowed for correct learner responses. For example, a flight simulator can provide within a few hours the equivalent of months of landing situations.

The safety factor. Often the required combination of behaviors in a task is too complex to be manipulated safely by a trainee. A simulator can be used therefore to separate elements of the tasks and to introduce new elements over time. In addition, emergency techniques can be learned and practiced without the disastrous consequences of failure to be found in an actual situation. In military, law enforcement, fire fighting, medical, and air transportation applications, the safety factor alone may be sufficient justification for simulators.

Incorporation of sound learning principles. Simulators permit the implementation of the principles of effective learning. Properly used, the simulator can introduce feedback, provide practice opportunities, and also enhance training transfer.

Newer training delivery technologies that extend these earlier approaches include computer-based training (CBT), Internet- and Intranet-based training delivery, interactive video, multimedia training, and distance learning. A common element in each of these approaches is the reliance on computers to deliver course content.

Computer-Based Training

Computer-based training (CBT), often called Computer-assisted training (CAI) as well, has a history nearly as long as that of the computer itself. Computer-based training models at first were confined to standalone or dedicated machines or to "dumb" terminals connected to a computer. Entire CBT courses could be copied onto floppy disks.

Today's computer-based training involves a wide array of multimedia technologies including sound, motion (video and animation), graphics, and hypertext. Some uses of these rich media still involve standalone workstations, but a much more common current solution is a networked multimedia computer laboratory with a server machine. These labs are often connected to the Internet as well, meaning that learners can access not only the information and programs on their workstations and the server, but can also gain entree to the entire World Wide Web. One of the biggest advantages of multimedia training is that in industries with high turnover rates, training can be executed more cost effectively—thus providing the right training at the right time to the right people (Greinsing-Pophal, 1998).

Early computer-based training approaches. Early CBT models, like their predecessors the teaching machines, used linear programs to introduce training content in a sequential fashion. Such programs used a drill-and-practice method. Later uses of CBT also included intrinsic or branching models. The growing capabilities of the computer allowed training program developers to create content in which the answer to one question dictated the next question presented to a learner, permitting individualization of the content. Students who responded correctly to the initial stimuli were presented a more difficult task while those who responded incorrectly were exposed to remedial material or a less difficult task.

Cooley and Glaser (1969) developed a generalized model of the elements involved in the creation of effective CBT systems:

- The goals of learning are specified in terms of observable learner behavior and the conditions under which the behavior is to be manifested.

- Initial capabilities of the learner are assessed at the beginning of the course of instruction.

- The learner selects (or is assigned) an educational alternative suited to his or her capability.

- The performance of the learner is monitored and continuously assessed throughout the learning process.

- The instruction progresses as a function of the interaction between the learner's performance, instructional alternatives, and criteria of competence.

- As instruction proceeds, data are gathered for monitoring and improving the instructional system.

One excellent example of a well-conceived and well-implemented CBT model is that of PLATO (for Programmed Logic for Automated Teaching Operations). The PLATO system includes capabilities for displays of all kinds, modifiable graphics, and touch-screen input. The system provides control and monitoring of student progress and the ability to maintain student and evaluation data. Topics as diverse as beginning math and reading, oscilloscope operation, and recipe preparation have been implemented via PLATO (Hurlock & Slough, 1976). The University of Illinois, the Federal Aviation Administration, and AT&T, among many other organizations, have used PLATO for training purposes for several decades.

Multimedia training. In the strictest sense, all training is "multimedia" in that it involves multiple senses. Learners exercise their hearing and sight as well as perform activities as part of their learning experience. The term *multimedia*, however, has a more exact meaning in the contemporary training context. Multimedia training is defined as training that uses a combination of audiovisual and computer-based technologies to provide content that includes text, graphics, animation, audio, and video. Because multimedia training uses computers, the trainee is able to interact with the content. The Internet or Intranet, standalone workstations with compact disk or Digital Versatile Disc (DVD) players, or interactive video systems can be used to deliver multimedia content.

Internet and Intranet training delivery. The individualization of courses has been given new life with the implementation of hypertext in Internet and other computer-based training programs. The learner is given control over the content, timing, and sequencing of course materials. Some of the many organizations embracing Internet-based training include CSX Transportation Inc., FlightSafety International, Xerox Management Institute, and the United States Air Force (Thornburg, 1998).

Both the commercialization and the popularization of the Internet began in the early 1990s with the advent of graphical user interfaces for browsing web content. The first such program, Mosaic, did for the Internet what Windows did for personal computers. It made the content of the web available in the form of rich media, beginning with graphics, and later including motion, sound, and three-dimensional images.

Many people today equate the Internet with the World Wide Web. In reality, the Internet is a much more generalized interconnected network of computer networks. Various protocols are used to share information, making such information readily available without respect to geographical or temporal boundaries. These protocols include the familiar HTTP (Hypertext Transfer Protocol) for displaying hypertext documents, FTP (File Transfer Protocol) for uploading and downloading files, Network News Transfer Protocol (NTTP) for access to Usenet Newsgroups, and protocols for electronic mail, text retrieval, and other purposes.

The ability to share text, graphics, animations, video, and audio content makes the Internet (or a private company's Intranet) an ideal medium not only for sharing information, but also for delivering training materials. An Intranet is a private network behind a "firewall," a software program that restricts use to company-authorized employees. Increasingly, web-browsing programs such as Netscape Navigator and Microsoft Internet Explorer are used to put a user-friendly face on Intranet content just as they are used to make Internet content more accessible.

For example, Lucent Technologies (formerly part of AT&T) provides company information, internal job postings, course listings, and some course content via the company Intranet. This approach is no longer the exclusive domain of large companies. Even small companies of one hundred or fewer employees are finding that an Intranet is an effective and efficient way to share information, to leverage training and other resources, and to distribute course content.

The use of the Internet and Intranets in training can be further subdivided into the categories shown in figure 4.2. The Internet (and a company Intranet) can be used to share information or to provide interaction between the instructor and the learner.

The approaches shown in figure 4.2 are cumulative. Each successively higher level of web-based training builds on the others. At the very highest level, the Internet is a medium providing a rich array of text, graphics, sounds, motion, and virtual reality along with access to additional online resources. At this level, the interaction between the learner and the technology is so great that each individual's learning experience is unique.

The Internet has revolutionized the delivery of training materials to remote locations. Electronic mail and instant messaging can allow participants to interact with each other and with the instructor. Chat rooms and videoconferencing can be used to enhance interactivity. Learners can access course handouts, review course materials, consult their instructor and other subject matter experts, and retrieve materials pertinent to their courses from servers around the world.

Emerging technologies for peer-to-peer file sharing, once the primary domain of music enthusiasts, are now finding learning and performance applications. These technologies, embodied in programs like Napster,

Figure 4.2
Levels of Web-Based Training

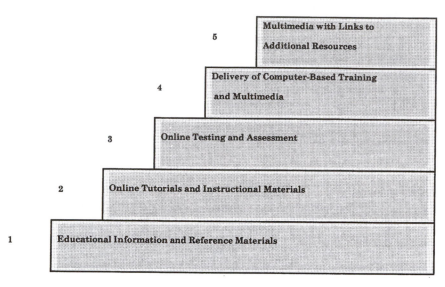

Based on: K. Kruse. Five levels of Internet-based training (1997), *Training and Development Journal*, 51 (2), pp. 60–61.

Scour Exchange, and iMesh, enable each computer connected to the Internet simultaneously to act as both a server and a client.

Audiovisual methods and interactive video. The use of audiovisual techniques to deliver instructional materials is as old as the motion picture camera. Soon after the invention of the movie camera, Frank Gilbreth, one of the earliest proponents and practitioners of the time and motion study, filmed tonsillectomies performed on his own children and then analyzed the film to find wasted time and motion in the surgical procedures. Gilbreth (who was immortalized along with his wife and business partner Lillian Gilbreth and their twelve children in the book and movie *Cheaper by the Dozen*) showed the film to the doctors, pointing out ways to improve the speed and efficiency of the operation.

The advent of the television and videotape provided another way to deliver educational materials over distance as well as to store the content for future and repeated use. Just as with motion pictures, television and videotapes provided one-way presentations without giving students a chance to interact with the instructor. Courses were broadcast by television and satellite, and stored on videotape for later viewing. Organizations like NTU, the National Technological University, began to offer college courses via video.

The merging of media made possible by faster computers and increased bandwidth has made accessible "streaming" audio and video from vendors such as Microsoft, Apple, and Real Media. The media files are "streamed" to the user's computer so that they can be played without being fully downloaded. With this technology, users can access full-motion video and CD-quality audio files delivered via the Internet or an Intranet from a server directly to the user's desktop or laptop computer.

Video has also become highly interactive through the development of videodisc, compressed video, and desktop videoconferencing technologies (Goldstein, 1993). These approaches allow the learner and the instructor or the learner and the system to interact, thereby creating an individualized real-time learning experience. Some products, such as the Instrux system are standalone-training stations with video cameras, optical disks, and computers integrated into a single device. Other video learning systems are networked via a local area network (LAN) or the Internet.

Interactive video training using optical disks, CD-ROMs, or DVDs providing full-motion video can present a situation in which the learner witnesses the correct use of a procedure or behavior. The learner can then attempt to duplicate the target behavior, with a video camera recording facial expressions as well as words. The session can be taped for feedback purposes and later critiqued by the course facilitator. Such training has been found to be highly effective in teaching sales and presentation skills.

Virtual and augmented reality. Virtual reality uses computers to provide trainees with a three-dimensional learning environment (Noe, 1999). Virtual reality permits the learner to use special devices or specially created computer displays to perceive and interact with the components of the learning environment (Adams, 1995). This type of training stimulates multiple senses and is therefore an extension of multimedia training. But in the case of virtual reality, the added elements of interactivity, tactile feedback, and other features create an artificial environment. In this artificial environment, the learner participates with the program.

Once the domain of science fiction, virtual reality is now used as an effective means of teaching complicated or dangerous tasks such as military operations and the robotic manufacturing of electronic equipment. Virtual environments have been used in such situations as the training of the team responsible for the launch and deployment of the Hubble Space Telescope, including the elements that were critical to the 1993 repair and replacement mission. In addition, the semiconductor industry is using virtual reality to simulate work environments inside PCs to help teach workers wafer inspection and clean-room practices, which can involve more than a hundred specific steps. Any mistake along the way can render an entire batch of chips useless, and virtual reality training has allowed these companies to provide comprehensive training at a much lower cost (Greengard, 1998). Further, a combination of biofeedback and virtual reality therapy has been used successfully to reduce fear of flying. Participants who experienced in artificial reality the takeoff and landing of airplanes were able to experience the actual events with far less stress and less expense than those who were taught by a traditional systematic desensitization approach ("Virtual reality," 1998).

One emerging technology is "augmented reality." Unlike virtual reality, which creates its own artificial environment, augmented reality superimposes additional information (text, sound, or graphics) upon the physical environment via special displays. This additional information can aid the trainee with decision-making or problem solving tasks. While virtual reality shuts out the physical environment to enable the learner to interact with the artificial environment, augmented reality overlays information, leaving the perception of the physical environment in place. By use of viewing devices or special clothing, a person can experience a heightened awareness of the features or characteristics of the environment that are important.

An initial application of augmented reality was the projection of navigational and weapon systems information onto the field of vision of military pilots. Other emerging applications include IBM's World Board, a viewer that looks much like a standard video camcorder. Using coordinates from an integrated Global Positioning System (GPS) interface, this high-tech viewer overlays relevant text, sound, and graphics onto the visual field as the user points the device. The World Board would have many possible uses, ranging from virtual tours of unfamiliar locations to law enforcement, military, and emergency medical applications. MIT researchers have developed prototype clothing that transmits signals from multiple body points. The so-called golf underwear can provide far richer feedback to the trainee than traditional videotape or computer programs (Hodgins, 2000), assisting the user, for instance, in making precise corrections to his or her golf swing.

Distance learning. Distance learning is not a new concept. The original distance learning courses were conducted through correspondence (Noe, 1999). Such courses persist to this day. Following correspondence courses, radio and television broadcast courses and audio and videotape sessions removed the distance between the instructor and the learner. Until recently, however, distance learning was a serial process with limited or delayed feedback to the learner. Today's distance learning technologies provide the opportunity for simultaneous interaction between the instructor and the trainee.

There are two basic distance education models. In *synchronous* distance learning, all trainees participate in a course at the same time and receive the course modules in sequence. An example of this type of distance education is the delivery of courses by compressed video from one site to another (or to multiple sites). Students at each remote site see and hear the instructor via television monitors and speakers. Learners can ask questions by pressing a switch on a microphone, and participants at both the local and remote sites are able to see and hear participants at other sites. Such synchronous distance learning models may involve expensive compressed video equipment and high bandwidth connections such as T1, cable, or DSL (Digital Subscriber Line) connections, or may involve ISDN (Integrated Systems Digital Network) lines and computer-based teleconferencing.

The major disadvantage of distance learning is the potential lack of interaction between the instructor and the far-site learner. Interaction among trainees is also an element that is a positive feature of classroom training, yet potentially missing from distance learning. When distance learning technologies are used simply to repackage and distribute "talking head" lectures without the opportunity for students to interact with each other and with the instructor, distance learning is probably no more likely to be effective than traditional lectures. It is important for designers and practitioners of distance learning to establish communication links between the trainer and the trainees (Noe, 1999). Onsite facilitators at a distance learning remote site should be available to answer questions, to demonstrate the use of the technology, and to moderate class sessions.

Recently, I had the opportunity to design and develop a distance education course in training and development. This course was taught at Louisiana State University-Shreveport and simultaneously transmitted to the University of New Orleans via compressed video technology. Students in the local classroom were able to see and interact with their counterparts at the remote site. Remote site students could see and hear the instructor and course presentations on large screen televisions. Students in both locations could ask questions by speaking into a microphone. Video cameras and display adapters at both locations could transmit visual images and computer screens.

As the course evolved through several offerings, other technologies were added to improve the information sharing, communication, and coordination between the sites. The first of these was a course web page, where students could access the course calendar, the syllabus, handouts, and resource materials. In addition to corresponding by electronic mail, the instructor created a virtual classroom with a chat room for online office hours. Students were encouraged to learn and use the compressed video technology for projects and class demonstrations. The compressed video technology permitted a combination of minilectures, slide presentations, demonstrations, exercises, guest speakers, and discussions involving learners at both locations. Students collaborated via the compressed video lab, the online chat room, and electronic mail. Course handouts were made available in advance of the classes via the course web page.

There were several occasions, however, when the technology failed to perform as expected, and only audio, fax, or telephone connected the remote site. In these cases, videotape was used to record the class session, and the tape was made available to the students at the remote site for independent viewing. The occasional failure of the technology pointed out the need for low-tech back-up strategies that would allow the course schedule to be met when the technology was unavailable.

The test performance of the remote site students was slightly better (though not statistically significantly so) than that of the students at the local site. Reaction measures (student ratings) of the course and instructor were uniformly high for both locations. In the instructor's experience, teaching a course by synchronous distance learning was challenging and fulfilling, but also a tremendous amount of work. To the extent possible, the author attempted to keep the technology used to transmit the course materials and to facilitate interactions "in the background." This goal was largely met, and a remote site facilitator helped immensely.

Asynchronous distance learning occurs when individual learners are able to complete course materials at their own rate. This type of learning is exemplified by courses, programs, and tutorials hosted on a web server and offered via the Internet (or a company Intranet). Different learners can complete the course modules at their own rate or even in different sequences. Web sites such as Hungry Minds (hungryminds.com) provide access to hundreds of online courses and tutorials, many of them free. In addition, expert advice can be found at Hungry Minds and sites like Askme.com. These resources are accessed and used by individuals in unique and personalized ways.

Distance learning in the information economy. Distance learning has become a big business. Corporations, government agencies, traditional colleges and universities, and for-profit educational institutions have seen the viability of offering courses and training curricula by distance learning technologies.

It is possible today to complete many course requirements and even to earn many undergraduate and graduate degrees via distance learning. For example, Capella University (based in Minneapolis) is a fully accredited "virtual campus" offering all its courses via distance learning technologies. Traditional brick-and-mortar classrooms are giving way to virtual colleges campuses. Many reputable traditional colleges and universities are now offering full or partial degree programs online. The growing list includes such notables as the University of Pennsylvania, Auburn University, the University of California, Indiana University, George Washington University, the University of Phoenix, the University of Maryland, and many others. The phenomenon of distance learning is not restricted to the United States. Internationally, such institutions as the Open University (in the United Kingdom) and many others also offer online degree programs.

Corporations such as AT&T, PriceWaterhouseCoopers, Motorola, Ford Motor Company, and many others are also finding distance learning (especially Internet- and Intranet-based courses) to be an effective way to deliver company-sponsored training. A good example of a profit-making organization involved in distance higher education is the Pangaea Network, a joint venture of Durand Communications, Inc., and Webb Interactive Services, Inc. Pangaea acquired the Electronic University Network (EUN) in 1998. EUN, working with various colleges and universities, offered the first online degree programs in 1986 (before the World Wide Web was even invented). EUN became the online education provider for America Online in 1992. Many of the institutions participating in EUN and now Pangaea are traditional public or private educational institutions.

Usage Rates of Various Delivery Technologies

Now that we have examined various training delivery technologies, an obvious question is how widely used the newer training delivery technologies are. In 1997 *Training* magazine published usage rates for some of the technologies discussed in this chapter. These usage rates are depicted in table 4.1.

Such surveys indicate that classroom training is still the predominant form but that newer technologies are gaining widespread acceptance. In particular, the computer is becoming a mainstay of the training department. These survey results must be interpreted with some amount of caution, however, since such practices as the implementation of networked computer laboratory classrooms could overlap several categories and may well have been included in the "classroom" category by the professionals surveyed.

The American Society for Training and Development addressed this issue in a 1998 study by surveying the percentage of training time involved with various training technologies (see table 4.2). These data present a slightly different picture, and as suspected, when training time is used, the

Table 4.1
Usage Rates of Instructional Methods

Training Method	Precent of Companies Using Each Method
Classroom	94%
Video	74%
Audiovisual	56%
Computer-Based Training on CD-ROM	36%
Computer-Based Training Using Intranet	21%
Computer-Based Training Using Internet	10%
Virtual Reality	3%

Source: Industry report 1997 (October 1997), *Training, 34*, 33–37.

Table 4.2
Usage Rates of Training Delivery Technologies

Precentage of Companies Using Each Method	Leading-Edge Companies	Entire Sample
Computer-based training	66%	35%
CD-ROM	44%	30%
Multimedia	31%	22%
EPSS	16%	7%
Intranet	13%	3%

Source: L.J. Bassi & M.E. Van Buren, The 1998 ASTD state of the industry report (1999), *Training and Development Journal: Supplemental Report*, 1, 3.

percentage of pure instructor-led classroom training was found to be less than in earlier surveys (Bassi & Van Buren, 1999). In the entire sample, instructor-led classroom training constituted 84 percent of the training time, whereas in leading-edge companies, the percentage was still a healthy 81 percent. The ASTD survey also showed that leading-edge companies are far more likely to use sophisticated training delivery technologies.

Evaluating Training Delivery Technologies

New technologies for training delivery should be evaluated carefully using (as a minimum) the following criteria:

- Learner Reactions
- Learning Outcomes Achieved
- Training Transfer Achieved
- Amount and Type of Continuing Support Available
- Cost Effectiveness

At a minimum, new training delivery methods should be compared with the two more traditional methods, classroom lecture and on-the-job training. Only if a new technology produces cost savings, productivity improvements, or enhanced learning outcomes as compared with the traditional approaches should the new technology be readily embraced. It is also important to assess the employees' readiness, to anticipate potential pitfalls, and to plan carefully for success (Hicks, 2000); if these items are neglected, a subsequent lack of management and employee support could easily materialize.

Indeed, it is both unfair and unwise to assume that because training materials employ new technology, they will be effective. As with any other type of training, the use of careful training needs analysis, the identification of desired outcomes, and the incorporation of sound learning principles can make or break a technology-rich training approach. According to Hartley (2000), some training departments have adopted technology without a thorough understanding of the business problems they were trying to address—just implementing "e-learning" to say they were doing so. To avoid this recipe for failure, trainers should have a solid understanding of why e-learning is a preferred platform in that e-learning tools are available 24-7 and knowledge can be "pushed to employees" just before they need to know it (Hartley, 2000).

Finally, it is important to note that new training technologies do not always live up to the promise of improved outcomes or lower costs. One fast food restaurant chain found, for example, that a multimedia training program for meal packing, though favorably received by employees, produced no better results than a less expensive approach using technical manuals and laminated instruction cards (Noe, 1999). Again, new training methods should be compared with classroom lecture and on-the-job training and only adopted if they produce cost savings, productivity improvements, and/or enhanced learning.

When to Choose New Training Delivery Technologies

It is important to understand that new training delivery technologies are extensions of traditional technologies. Virtual and augmented reality is an extension of mechanical simulators. The Internet and Intranets and interactive video are technological enhancements to traditional classroom and on-the-job training. According to Noe (1999), new training technologies should be considered under several conditions, which are expanded upon in the following section.

- There is ample funding provided to develop and use the new technology.

- Trainees are geographically separated and travel costs related to training are high.

- Trainees are untroubled by and skilled in the use of the new technology.

- The increased use of the new technology is aligned with the organization's business strategy.

- Employees would have an arduous task in attending prescheduled training programs.

- Current training methods permit limited practice, reinforcement, and evaluation opportunities.

Funding. New technology can be expensive. Furthermore, adding realism via technology increases the price tag. Training departments may find ultimately that the use of new technology allows the reduction of training staff, but this cannot happen without an initial investment in hardware, software, and training. Many organizational leaders understand and budget for the equipment and software, but these costs are essentially the down payment. The cost of training the trainers who will use the new technology, while large, is surpassed only by the cost of not training these new users.

Training costs. A typical scenario for a geographically dispersed organization is to send instructors to remote sites, and to send trainees to centralized training centers. Travel costs include transportation, lodging, and meals. These costs must be added to the costs of time away from the job, trainers' salaries, and the costs of maintaining training facilities.

A cost-benefit analysis can be used to determine whether companies can save money by making some of their courses available via the Internet or the Intranet. While costs of equipment, software, and training in the use of the technology are still applicable, with such courses, travel costs and lost productivity costs should be reduced.

An emerging trend to lower training costs is the development of regional web-based training centers such as that being developed by the City of Phoenix Water Services Department. Combining university, municipal, and corporate training resources, these centers can provide online courses to city employees and to other organizations on a fee-sharing or subscription basis. Similar approaches are being explored by the cities of Toronto, Akron, and others. The advantage of the regional training center is quickly apparent when one considers the alternative. Three different courses delivered by traditional methods to three different clients would involve nine separate trips (of the instructor to the site or of the learners to the classroom). The same three courses offered online would incur no travel costs.

A network of regional web-based training centers, working much as the hub-and-spoke system of the U.S. Airlines, could be envisioned. As shown in figure 4.3, such centers would allow smaller organizations without the funding or means of developing their own courses to participate in web-based courses for a fraction of the cost of traditional courses.

Trainee preparation. Trainees should not be expected to learn new technology while they are learning new subject matter (unless, of course, the technology is the subject matter). Until such time as technology is fully embedded and largely invisible, the organization should invest in orientation, equipment training, and coaching to familiarize employees with new technology.

Training as a strategy. For many organizations, technology is seen as a risk, and training is considered to be a necessary evil. In these organizations, technology and training are both likely to be undervalued and undercapitalized. Sophisticated organizations, however, are much more likely to

Figure 4.3
Regional Web-Based Training Center Concept

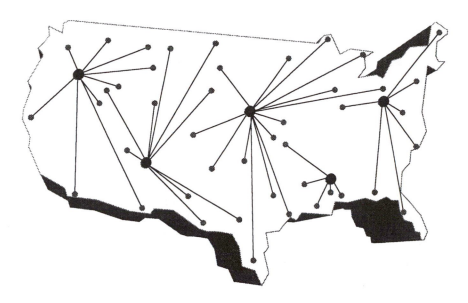

see both training and technology as strategic weapons capable of creating a sustainable competitive advantage.

Scheduling considerations. The present author once left home (Shreveport, Louisiana) and flew first to Dallas and then to Phoenix for a two-hour meeting—at the insistence and expense of a client—and at noon, flew back by way of Dallas, arriving home by midnight. This schedule resulted in a loss of six hours of work productivity and eight hours of personal time. Either videoconferencing or an audio conference call could have accomplished much of the purpose of the face-to-face meeting at a far smaller total cost. Similarly, a knowledge worker who takes an Internet-based course or participates in a team meeting via groupware at his or her own desk for two hours would be able to achieve productive outcomes for the rest of the workday. The heavy workload of air traffic controllers and the difficulty in scheduling offsite training were major factors in the decision by the Federal Aviation Administration (FAA) to use the PLATO system for training.

Practice and feedback. Many programs offer little by way of practice and feedback. This often leads to the "vanishing training phenomenon" in which the new skill fails to transfer to the work environment. While new technology will not automatically overcome poor training transfer, the possibility exists through careful design and implementation to improve transfer and to build reinforcement for newly acquired skills into the workplace. Technologically enriched training can also provide assessments of performance and offer corrective coaching. An especially powerful tool is the implementation of Electronic Performance Support Systems (EPSS) or Intelligent Tutoring Systems as mechanisms for follow-up skill enhancement, reinforcement, and refresher training. These tools will be addressed more completely in a later section.

Bottom Line Evidence on Advanced Training Delivery Techniques

At this point in the discussion, it is imperative to generate some kind of understanding about the research findings on the effectiveness of newer training technologies. Put simply, advanced training technologies have a mixed track record. A number of studies found that programmed instruction is typically faster than instructor-led courses while producing the same or more effective results (Hall & Freda, 1982). Yet other studies have found that new technology produces no better results than traditional methods (Noe, 1999). When transfer and retention are examined, new training delivery technologies are usually found to be comparable with traditional training (Noe, 1999), though there is some speculation that training support technologies such as expert systems and Electronic Performance Support systems should enhance transfer and retention.

One newer training technology that has received specific attention by researchers is distance learning. Distance learning technology has been studied extensively, and the results of more than three hundred studies indicate that distance learning produces learning outcomes that are not significantly different from those produced by traditional methods (Russell, 1999). However, most likely because of the limited interaction between the instructor and the learner, distance learning often produces less favorable reaction measures than traditional classroom training.

TRAINING PROGRAM DESIGN TECHNOLOGIES

The use of the computer and other new technologies is not limited to training delivery. Training developers are finding that software packages such as Designer's Edge by Allen Communication can assist in tasks ranging from training needs analysis to multimedia curriculum development. Designer's Edge automates many of the tasks associated with needs analysis, consideration of delivery alternatives, and curriculum design. This tool also standardizes design terminology and documentation, improving the quality and consistency of the curricula designed by different course authors.

Course developers can make use of a variety of computer programs to create visually attractive and easily updated course manuals. Course presentation materials and handouts are often developed by use of such programs as Microsoft PowerPoint. These electronic documents can be updated easily; they can also be distributed and stored electronically on a company web server or the Internet for easy access by remote course participants.

TRAINING ADMINISTRATION TECHNOLOGIES

The collection and administration of training records, course enrollments, testing and certification, the planning and publication of course catalogs, and the linkage of training information with other company data are all elements of training administration. Additionally, many corporate training departments are assuming the role of brokers of external training providers. This implies that another major activity of training administration is the creation and maintenance of a database of training vendors. Training administration historically was labor-intensive and largely paper-based. New imaging applications, interactive voice technologies, and software applications are making training administration both more effective and more efficient, as discussed next.

Imaging applications. Imaging applications involve the scanning of documents for electronic storage and retrieval. Optical character recognition (OCR) software applications allow scanned documents to be searched by keywords. Imaging permits quicker retrieval and more compact storage than paper-based filing and retrieval. Training records, certificates, and other documents can be scanned and stored. Documents can be retrieved and printed as necessary.

Interactive voice technologies. Using personal computers and voice-response systems, training departments can enable learners to enroll themselves in courses, get information on courses and prerequisites, and speak to a staff member if they have questions. Such technologies can be used to supplement Intranet-based course catalogs, course descriptions, and course enrollments. Many colleges allow students to complete course registration via telephone or the Internet. The registration systems can be programmed to block students without course prerequisites from enrolling in advanced courses, yet these systems may not adequately replace the face-to-face advising that is helpful to students as they plan their course schedules. Similar problems in a corporate setting may surface if essential supervisor-trainee discussions are bypassed before an employee enrolls in a program.

Software applications. Information including training records, employee transcripts, certified skills, educational experience, classroom capacities, instructor schedules, and many other types of data can be gathered, stored, and retrieved through automated systems. The administrators of small training departments may find that programs such as Microsoft Access could serve as effective relational database management programs for training records.

For larger training departments, such programs as Training Register can be used for end-to-end training record management. Other administration tools (for example, Manage-It!) allow trainers to register participants, to record exam results, and to monitor learning progress. Furthermore, there are test development systems (for example, Ace-It!) where trainers can enter questions into templates to create a variety of tests or exams, complete with graphics, photos, feedback, and so on (Miller, 1998).

A growing trend is for training records to be linked to "enterprise software" such as the program R3 from vendor SAP. Enterprise software provides a completely integrated information system, which allows human resource development and deployment more effectively to be part of the planning and strategy of the organization. Many of these enterprise programs have training or human resource information modules. Such programs allow training records such as mastery or certification to be correlated with job performance, quality, safety, and other outcomes. Additionally, planning and cost control become more effective as training information is integrated with other company data.

Internet- or Intranet-based software can be used to provide employees access to training information. Such data might include individual training records, available programs or courses and descriptions, access to educational partners, tuition assistance, and other information. For example, the city of Tempe, Arizona, plans to make such information available to city employees via the Internet. The training records available online will replace hard copy transcripts that must currently be printed and mailed or faxed to employees. City employees can find course descriptions, prerequisites, and enrollment forms online at the city web site.

TRAINING SUPPORT TECHNOLOGIES

Lastly, there are technologies that are available to trainers and trainees to help support training-related activities and to improve retention and training transfer. Each is discussed in turn.

Expert Systems

Expert systems organize and apply the knowledge of human experts to specific problems. These systems are usually software-based. Expert systems have three elements (Noe, 1999):

- A base of knowledge that contains information about a specific subject.
- A decision-making ability that imitates an expert's reasoning to draw conclusions from the knowledge base to solve problems and answer questions.
- An interface that allows the user to provide and receive information from expert systems.

Xerox Corporation, for example, developed an expert system called FRED to capture the knowledge and wisdom of an employee who was the resident guru on developing spare parts strategies for new products. The employee, also named Fred, was soon to retire, and none of his coworkers had his depth and breadth of experience and knowledge. Fred was interviewed extensively, and his decision rules were codified in a software program named after him. Less experienced Xerox workers in product delivery teams could consult Fred's expert knowledge when developing spare parts approaches for the products being designed.

In addition to their ability to support training, expert systems are used as training delivery mechanisms as well. By learning the expert's decision rules, the employee is also learning to avoid costly mistakes or omissions. The expert system can also help employees avoid decision bias or idiosyncrasies.

Groupware

Due to the increased use of distributed work groups in which experts and stakeholders are geographically dispersed and horizontal interaction is required to address complex problems, groupware is gaining more visibility and usage in the workplace. Groupware facilitates consensus building, idea generation, information sharing, voting, and problem solving tasks. Groupware packages may involve computer-mediated communication, shared virtual space, web-based conferencing, interactive video, and other technologies.

Specifically, group support systems (GSS) are designed to store, analyze, display, and facilitate the electronic exchange of multiple-user information. In this way, GSS technology provides the technological tools necessary for communicating between group members, structuring the decision-making process, and keeping records of individual input (Dennis & Gallupe, 1993). GSS, for example, can be used to rapidly encode and process information—notes can be tallied, anonymous comments can be categorized and reviewed, and ideas and plans can be efficiently generated. These tools could be especially helpful in case-oriented management development programs.

Intelligent Tutoring Systems

Intelligent Tutoring Systems make use of artificial intelligence to provide tutoring, coaching, or empowering learning environments (Steele-Johnson & Hyde, 1997). Tutoring attempts to increase trainees' content knowledge and understanding. Coaching provides artificial environments in which the trainee can practice new skills. And empowerment refers to the learner's ability to explore freely the content of the training program (Noe, 1999). Intelligent Tutoring Systems make use of virtual reality and artificial intelligence to accomplish the following (Steele-Johnson & Hyde, 1997):

- match instruction to individual learner needs

- communicate with and respond to the learner

- model the trainee's learning process

- decide, on the basis of a trainee's previous performance, what information to provide

- make decisions about the trainee's level of understanding

- conduct self-assessments that result in modifications to the teaching process

Electronic Performance Support Systems

An Electronic Performance Support System (EPSS) is a computer application that provides on request information, advice, or skills training. Employees can consult the EPSS when they have problems or decisions they feel exceed their current level of knowledge or skill, or if they are unsure of the accuracy of their diagnosis of the situation (Noe, 1999). This electronic version of on-the-job training is usually only a mouse click or a press of the F1 key away from the user. EPSSs are considered to be an "embedded" technology since they are resident with the parent program.

Modern software programs typically include "wizards," or self-instructional programs, that walk the user through an application or a feature of the software. A familiar example of an EPSS is the Microsoft Windows Office Assistant, the paper clip character that pops up to offer support and advice for tasks ranging from typing a letter to sending a fax to creating a spreadsheet. This same approach could be applied in corporate training scenarios to aid employees back on the job when trying to employ trained skills, especially for those employees responsible for knowing voluminous amounts of data that change frequently.

Other performance support options provide employees with just-in-time coaching, performance assessment, and access to developmental activities and tools to manage professional development (Miller, 1998). For example, Asymetrix Librarian, from Asymetrix Learning Systems Inc. of Bellevue, Washington, allows firms to assign an employee to a specified situation, such as overcoming resistance to change, or to a specific skill, such as conflict management. Then, the employer tracks the trainee's completion of assignments and runs training-tracking reports.

The New Trend: Combining Learning and Performance to Achieve High Impact

Technologies such as groupware and EPSSs are blending the distinction between training and working. The worker, in the process of doing his or her job, is also learning. The technology that supports also teaches, and the worker who learns performs at the same time.

This trend of combining learning with performance and training with technology shows no sign of abatement. Furthermore, this recent movement supports "the placement of training closest to the job." Given consistently voiced supervisory concerns regarding employees being "sent away" to training programs, removing them from their workplace, this is an important new emphasis in corporate training. In sum, as training technology continues to be embedded in the work performance environment, distinctions between expert systems, intelligent tutoring systems, groupware, and performance support systems will cease.

LOOKING INTO THE FUTURE: TRAINING AND TECHNOLOGY

Heretofore, technology has been a "foreground" item in training. When comparing methods of training, the learner, instructor, and researcher alike concentrate on the differences in technology. In the future, technology will fade into the background and become more entrenched into the learning experience, becoming a transparent feature of the training. The faster and more powerful computers become, the easier they are to use, and therefore, the more likely computers and computer-based technologies are to be employed in training design, delivery, support, and administration.

A far-reaching analysis sponsored by the American Society for Training & Development and the National Governor's Association speculated on the present and future of technology in training. The projected role of technology in future training is displayed in table 4.3.

Technology will "take center stage" less often as learners use it without having to think about it. Much the same way as electric motors were embedded in appliances and in the process became invisible, computer technology is "disappearing." Ultimately, generations of learners and workers familiar with computers for their entire lives should make this transformation faster. However, many adult learners may continue to struggle to keep up with their younger counterparts. In fact, it has been recognized that some learners still prefer classroom instruction (Ouellette, 1999; Wells, 1999).

Nonetheless, virtual reality has paved the way for augmented reality in the sense that computer simulated environments have been found to be engaging. In fact, virtual reality and simulators have actually been found to cause motion sickness, disorientation, and other problems generically

Table 4.3
Training Technology: Today and Tomorrow

Today	Tomorrow
Technology in the foreground	Technology in the background— Transparent, embedded
Smart technology	Intelligent technology (learns in use)
Virtual	Augmented
Artificial intelligence	Augmented intelligence
Generic	Task-specific
Good guesses	Precision predictability
Preprogrammed	Adaptive to user and situation
Proprietary	Open standards

Adapted from: H.W. Hodgins, Into the future: A vision paper (2000), *American Society for Training & Development and the National Governor's Association Commission on Technology and Adult Learning*, Washington, DC: American Society for Training & Development.

known as "simulator sickness" (Noe, 1999). But just as the technology is becoming embedded in the training environment, it will be used more often to supplement or augment reality rather than to replace it with an artificial substitute.

According to the vision of ASTD and the National Governor's Association, ultimately technology will largely obviate the need for event-based training. The notion of the classroom will extend beyond even the personal computer or workstation. Personal "training assistants" and "intelligent tutors" can be combined, for example, with augmented reality in the *actual* work performance environment to anticipate one's next move, to offer advice, and even to provide a demonstration of the correct procedure.

Just as augmented reality will surpass virtual reality, augmented intelligence will go beyond artificial intelligence. By making these technologies immediately and widely available, organizations will provide instant learning opportunities, again reducing the need for off-the-job training. For example, imagine an emergency surgery where the medical student is actually guided by augmented intelligence and augmented reality as images of her own hands correctly demonstrate the next step in the procedure (Hodgins, 2000).

SUMMARY AND CONCLUSIONS

Technology and training have become inseparable. Technology is used to design, deliver, administer, and support training programs. Today, however, the role of technology in training is very much in the foreground. The training technologies often have to be conquered themselves before trainers and learners can use them effectively.

The future holds the promise of technology that is embedded and invisible to the user. More important, the distinction between learning and performing is becoming blurred. The ASTD and National Governor's Association describe the combination of performing, capturing knowledge, managing, and learning into a new state of "learnativity," which author H. Wayne Hodgins defines as the intersection of learning, creativity, and productivity. In this state, learning and working are a synchronous activity.

As learning and working merge, technology will be seamlessly integrated into the web of employees' work-learning environment. This assimilation will enable trainers, training managers, and training designers to concentrate on learning rather than on technology.

BIBLIOGRAPHY

Adams, N. (1995, June). Lessons from the virtual world. *Training*, 45–48.

Bassi, L.J., & Van Buren, M.E. (1999). The 1998 ASTD State of the Industry Report. *Training and Development Journal*. Supplement, 1, 3.

Brown, R. & Hernstein, R.J. (1975). *Psychology*. Boston: Little, Brown.

Cooley, W.W., & Glaser, R. (1969). The computer and individualized instruction. *Science*, 166, 574–582.

Dennis, A.R., & Gallupe, R.B. (1993). A history of group support systems empirical research: Lessons learned and future directions. In L.M. Jessup & J.S. Valacich (Eds.), *Group Support Systems: New Perspectives* (pp. 59–77). New York: Macmillan Publishing Company.

Goldstein, I.L. (1993). *Training in organizations*. (3rd ed.). Pacific Grove, CA: Brooks-Cole.

Greengard, S. (1998, January 19). "Virtual" training becomes reality. *Industry Week*, 72–76.

Greinsing-Pophal, L. (1998, May). Multimedia training technology. *HR Magazine Supplement: Focus on HR Technology*, 16–21.

Hall, E.R., & Freda, J.S. (1982). *A comparison of individualized and conventional instruction in navy technical training: Technical report no. 117*. Orlando, FL: Training Analysis and Evaluation Group.

Hartley, D. (2000). All aboard the e-learning train. *Training and Development Journal*, 54(7), 37–42.

Hicks, S. (2000). First-time WBT. *Training and Development Journal*, 54(6), 75.

Hodgins, H.W. (2000). *Into the future: A vision paper*. American Society for Training & Development and the National Governor's Association Commission on Technology and Adult Learning. Washington, DC: American Society for Training & Development.

Hurlock, R.E., & Slough, D.A. (1976). Experimental evaluation of PLATO IV technology: Final report. *NPRDC technological report 76TQ-44*. San Diego: Navy Personnel Research Studies and Technology.

Industry Report 1997. (1997, October) *Training*, 33–37.

Kruse, K. (1997). Five levels of internet-based training. *Training and Development Journal, 51(2)*, 60–61.

Miller, L. (1998, December). What's new? *HR Magazine*, S14–S15.

Noe, R.A. (1999). *Employee training & development*. New York: Irwin McGraw-Hill.

Ouellette, T. (1999, April 26). Training: Pros and cons. *Computerworld*, 61–62.

Pressey, S.L. (1950). Development and appraisal of devices providing immediate automatic scoring of objective tests and concomitant self-instruction. *Journal of Psychology, 29*, 417–447.

Russell, T.L. (1999). *The no significant difference phenomenon*. Raleigh: North Carolina State University Press.

Skinner, B.F. (1954). Science of learning and the art of teaching. *Harvard Educational Review, 24*, 86–97.

Steele-Johnson, D., & Hyde, B.G. (1997). Advanced technologies in training: Intelligent tutoring systems and virtual reality. In M.A. Quinones & A. Ehrenstein (Eds.), *Training for a Rapidly Changing Workplace* (pp. 225–248). Washington, DC: American Psychological Association.

The 1997 National HRD Executive Survey. (1997). Washington, DC: American Society for Training and Development.

Thornburg, L. (1998, January). Investment in training technology yields good returns. *HR Magazine*, 37–41.

Virtual reality therapy for fear of flying. (1998). *Telemedicine and Virtual Reality, 3*, 113.

Wells, R.C. (1999, March). Back to the (internet) classroom. *Training*, 50–54.

Chapter 5

Training Transfer: Ensuring Training Gets Used on the Job

Lisa A. Burke

Most of us are likely familiar with, and maybe somewhat perplexed by, the training issue discussed in this chapter. Certainly, the leading training and development magazines and journals, and the various sessions at leading training conferences, give ample attention to the issue. Moreover, it affects any trainer, consultant, manager, or professional who works in the training field. The issue is transfer of training, or the long-term use of trained knowledge, skills, and abilities back on the job.

When positive transfer occurs, trainees are actually using on the job what they have learned in training. The idea, therefore, is that training should induce some type of long-term change in the individual. The essential ingredients of positive transfer include: (1) a presumption of learning in training; (2) the application of the trained knowledge and skills on the job; and (3) some assessment of the knowledge and skills as effective and maintained over a reasonable time period (Newstrom, 1986). In contrast, zero transfer implies that the training intervention had no effect—in other words, the training was a waste of time, money, and resources for the organization. And in the worst case scenario, negative transfer suggests an inhibiting effect of training on job performance, such that the trainees come back to the job and actually perform worse.

Disconcerting estimates of transfer rates have been cited throughout the training literature. Most commonly, it is proposed that trainees use a disappointing 10 to 15 percent of their training one year after attending formal programs (Tyler, 2000). In one specific study, training specialists indicated that retention rates approach a meager 40 percent immediately after management training programs, 25 percent at six months, and 15 percent at one year (Newstrom, 1986). Granted, the validity of any of these estimates, and how they were formulated, could be questioned. But even if the actual rate of transfer is 15 percent, 25 percent, or even 35 percent one year after a program, is this a reality that any of us is comfortable with?

Given that corporate training is a multibillion dollar industry in our country, this hardly appears to be an issue to gloss over. Furthermore, this documented transfer problem greatly dilutes a firm's return on investment, lessens trainers' credibility with line managers, and promotes a "training is a waste of my time" mentality amongst trainees. Frankly, these are outcomes that training professionals and organizations can no longer afford to neglect, overlook, or put at the bottom of the priority list.

In this chapter, reasons why the transfer problem is often ignored in organizations is discussed, along with the various factors that influence transfer, and finally, some of the more successful and effective transfer interventions. In addition, a simplified framework is advanced for tackling the transfer dilemma. It outlines specific and practical actions that trainers, trainees, and managers can take (before, during, and after programs) to effectively increase the extent to which trainees use training when they return to their jobs. Finally, a practical model for measuring transfer rates is reviewed.

IS TRANSFER TROUBLING TRAINERS ENOUGH?

An obvious question that surrounds this issue is, Why do some managers, some trainers, and some training departments prefer to look the other way or even totally ignore the documented transfer problem? Similar to a computer virus, if undetected and not addressed, the transfer problem will escalate and wreak havoc throughout the performance management system. Thus, this training issue is very real, and the reverberating effects of not addressing it are pervasive. Let's consider the various reasons behind managers' neglect of this critical training and development issue.

To the extent an organization disregards employee development as a priority, discounts training evaluation, or places training in the background, then of course, training personnel will respond in kind to the larger context. Put simply, a trainer's priorities tend to reflect the organization's priorities. If top managers really do not see training as a vital activity, or view training as an organizational cost and not as an investment, then training will take the proverbial back seat. This attitude will, in turn, invariably infiltrate the training department. Similarly, if a firm uses the training department as a landing place for employees who can't cut it anywhere else in the organization, the implicit message is "We don't really care about training—it's an unnecessary appendage."

Perhaps the transfer problem goes unattended to because some top managers aren't savvy enough to impose a level of accountability on the training function. Clearly (and unfortunately!), not all senior managers have had human resource training and/or functional human resource job experience. When senior managers are not aware of the sophistication that the training function has reached, they are unlikely to place full demands on their training staff (that is, to ask for documentation of training outcomes, etc). And in these situations, trainers will continue to produce a product that commands little respect and that serves minimal ends, and top managers will essentially be throwing money down the drain.

Other top managers are probably sharp enough but for whatever reason fail to make training and training transfer a priority. Some, plain and simple, just don't care. Others may not really want to learn the extent of the transfer problem for fear of exposing "the rotten egg." Indeed, if a grave transfer problem were to be exposed, it would be one more thing for them to deal with, which simply may not top their priority list. Granted, many things compete for top manager priorities in the new business reality, and senior managers are under much stress in coping with the competitive climate.

However, the most effective organizations will (at least) hire training personnel who are skilled in the science of training and development (or who have the ability to learn) and then give them the following charge: "Whatever you do should be needed in *this* organization, effectively designed and instructed, and most importantly, used!" This concise directive would help tremendously to let trainers know that the top management team (a) is knowledgeable about the value of training interventions and progressive training practices, (b) cares about employee and organizational development, and (c) is inclined to expect and/or measure results.

For sure, leading edge training departments and trainers worth their salt do not regard transfer as an afterthought; they realize that transfer pervades every aspect of the training system, including needs assessment, the creation of learning objectives, program design, program delivery, and program evaluation. In other words, these trainers realize that the transfer problem should be addressed throughout the entire training process and are ready to tackle it head on. And if someone were to ask them to define the transfer problem, to discuss potential root causes, and to outline their action plan for dealing with it, they would have very little difficulty in responding.

Yet trainers cannot wait to be asked! That is, in all fairness, we cannot solely attribute the neglect of training transfer to an organization's line managers. Often (and perhaps even more frequently) training personnel themselves do a poor job in assertively communicating to managers how training could help solve their performance problems. In these instances, there can be no finger-pointing, and trainers need to assume more accountability for transfer neglect.

In the end, regardless of the reason the transfer problem is played down in firms, it still persists and requires concerted attention. If transfer is not being addressed in your organization, do some analysis to figure out why—then take action. To help in framing your actions, a model of the various influences affecting training transfer is developed in the next section and examined.

A WHOLE HOST OF POTENTIAL CAUSES

Certainly, one of the most frustrating elements inhibiting transfer is the fact that so many factors influence it. It is so easy to become overwhelmed by these numerous and potential causes. However, one useful approach is to classify the whole host of possible causes as occurring before, during, and/after the training intervention. This simplified model gives us a place to start in our thinking about transfer and is easy to conceptualize.

Figure 5.1 is a longitudinal, systems-oriented model of important variables in the training process that influence transfer outcomes. This model represents a synthesis of the more prominent transfer research (Baldwin &

Figure 5.1
Training Transfer Model

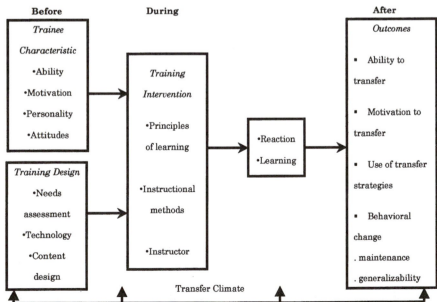

Ford, 1988; Burke, 1996; Tannenbaum, Cannon-Bowers, Salas, & Mathieu, 1993) and illustrates how deeply rooted the transfer problem can be throughout a training system and organization's culture, values, policies, and practices.

To summarize the model, we see that there are numerous factors before, during, and after training that may influence transfer outcomes either directly or indirectly via their effects on learning. In general, these factors can be related to those elements that a trainee brings to the training situation, those related to the training intervention itself, and those stemming from the context in which the training occurs. Let us next turn to a discussion of each of the model's components.

Trainee Characteristics

In terms of trainee characteristics, individuals coming into a training intervention have a varying ability and motivation level, set of attitudes, and personality that will affect their performance before, during, and after the program. At the most basic level, trainees must have the ability to learn. Surprisingly, in some employee cohorts, basic skill deficiencies in reading and writing can pose serious threats to learning. For example, in a recent guest lecture during my training and development course, a training director relayed that in the manufacturing division of her company, increasing efforts are being used to ensure that the people they hire possess basic verbal skills (or at least the ability and motivation to learn). The firm was finding that numerous individuals would approach trainers after attending a session to reveal their inability to read beyond a certain level or even to read at all. In fact, this training director is currently seeking a workplace literacy program from a local university to help with this pronounced problem.

At the same time, should trainees be unmotivated to learn the new skills in the training program, transfer will be minimized. Why are some individuals not motivated to learn in training? It may be due to lack of support from bosses, an unclear WIIFM (what's in it for me), lack of time, or work overload. Or perhaps they feel that their time is better spent on the job or they don't perceive the need for skill improvement. Ironically, these are typically the employees who most need training! Regardless, many of these motivational variables stem from and/or are related to larger contextual influences in the firm, which will be discussed in detail later in this chapter.

Employee attitudes may also be a cause of low transfer rates in a firm if employees and trainees have, for example, low job satisfaction, minimal organizational commitment, and/or intentions to leave the firm. These types of job attitudes are generally attributable to the larger organizational context, such as the degree of support from their direct supervisor and/or peers and the nature of their work. Once again, there is a strong need for "doing many other things right" in order to make a training intervention effective.

Finally, individual personality can play a role in training transfer. Individuals who are high on the trait of "openness to experience" have repeatedly and consistently demonstrated higher performance in training programs (Mount & Barrick, 1995). This means that people who are curious, open to learning new things, and willing to dive into a learning situation are likely to produce a high return on the firm's training investment. Additionally, conscientiousness has been evidenced as the most consistent and universal personality-based predictor of general job performance (Barrick, Mount, & Strauss, 1993). As such, managers have been advised to recruit and select only the most disciplined and responsible set of applicants. Such personality traits can be measured by trainers with personality inventories, such as the *Personality Characteristics Inventory* (PCI), the *NEO Personality Inventory*, or the *Hogan Personality Inventory* (HPI). While we think of these tests as typically used by the staffing department, perhaps trainers should be equally interested in their use to enhance transfer.

Training Design

Training interventions must also be designed effectively in order to enhance transfer. In part, this is done by conducting an effective needs assessments, as discussed in an earlier chapter. Clearly, it is important for trainers, supervisors, and trainees to understand why training is needed and what specific learning objectives are targeted for improvement. Skipping this step in the training process neglects the level of sophistication that training design has reached. However, some times organizations skip this essential first step to save time and money or because they are absolutely convinced that they know what type of training is needed and who needs it. This is unfortunate because the ultimate training, in these situations, is likely less effective or possibly not even needed at all, which is obviously a waste of money.

Nonetheless, training content must be relevant and logically sequenced, as part of the program design phase. More organizations are consequently hiring instructional systems designers in their training staffs (or contracting with them externally) because these professionals are trained in how to effectively design a training intervention. Simply put, there is a "science" to this training and development stuff. My advice is to either learn it or hire someone.

Lastly, advanced technologies should be used to enhance transfer. Not surprisingly, the chapter on training technologies informs the present discussion. Technology can be used during the training program to appeal to a broader array of learning styles and to ensure content clarity and learning. Furthermore, there are exciting new technologies that can aid transfer by digitizing job aids for trainees' use (for example, Electronic Performance Support Systems, discussed in the preceding chapter). In this technology era, trainers will either get on the technology bandwagon, or their training interventions, employee learning, and organizational performance will suffer the consequences.

Transfer Climate

Probably one of the more critical influences on the retention and use of trained skills back on the job is transfer climate (Rouiller and Goldstein, 1993). Recent research is consistently finding that transfer climate plays a key role in the training process, and due to its pervasive impact on transfer, transfer climate is depicted in figure 5.1 as influencing learning and retention throughout the entire model. This indicates its importance in the present discussion.

Transfer climate refers to the perceptions that describe characteristics of the work environment that facilitate or inhibit the use of trained skills. According to Rouiller and Goldstein's original work in this area, two general dimensions of transfer climate include (a) the situations trainees encounter as well as (b) the consequences they experience when applying training to the job. Both signify to employees what is important in their work context, thereby influencing trainees' transfer of training. A situation cue is anything that encourages trainees to use what has been learned in training (for example, a discussion with a supervisor regarding application of program skills) and a consequence is anything that happens to trainees as a result of either using or not using the trained skills on the job (for example, receiving praise from supervisors for demonstrating skill improvement on the job).

According to Burke and Baldwin (1999), the major factors around which transfer climate measurement items cluster include (1) immediate supervisory influence/involvement, (2) general attitudes toward training, and (3) training policies and practices. These three elements compose transfer climate and therefore deserve marked practitioner attention. More specifically, the types of behaviors, attitudes, and values that reflect these dimensions include, but are not limited, to the following:

- Supervisors show interest in what trainees learn in training.
- Trainees regularly discuss their training needs and developmental plans to meet those needs with their supervisor.
- Supervisors expect trainees to make use of their newly trained skills on the job.
- Supervisors encourage trainees to describe new techniques to other employees.
- Values or attitudes promoted in training are consistent with values on the job.
- Supervisors pay more than lip service to the value and usefulness of training.

- Supervisors select training programs for employees based on established criteria and an employee's training needs.
- Trainees meet with supervisors to discuss objectives of programs they attend.
- Training is linked to strategic plans and objectives.
- Training efforts are evaluated for their return on investment.

Training professionals can administer transfer climate surveys to individual trainees and/or to key informants in their firm (for example, training and development departmental personnel) to get some kind of indication as to the favorableness of the transfer climate their trainees face. Trainers can then use transfer climate survey results to (a) create organizational development interventions for improving transfer climate, and/or (b) customize posttraining transfer interventions. These interventions are discussed more in the implications section of this chapter.

The first factor that accounted for the most variance in the Burke and Baldwin study was, not surprisingly, immediate supervisory involvement and influence. The savvy trainer knows he or she can achieve little if line supervisors are not supportive of training. Glancing through the aforementioned items reveals those attitudes, behaviors, and values that work to produce a positive or favorable transfer climate. In essence, transfer climate taps the degree to which an organization has sophisticated training practices and values and rewards individual growth and development.

Again, transfer climate influences trainees before, during, and after a training intervention. Thus, if a boss recognizes the value of skill enhancement, discusses expectations for an employee's learning, nominates the employee for programs that address important skill deficits, and holds her accountable for using training on the job, then she will likely go into the program with an open attitude and willingness to learn. During the training, she will probably be more actively engaged and participative—taking notes, generating action plans, and interacting with instructors to enhance her learning and to help her solve work problems. And perhaps most importantly, after the training, she will be prepared to discuss the program with her supervisor, share her training materials, discuss her learning, and/or share her knowledge in a briefing with coworkers. This is what a positive transfer climate does, and therefore its role is vital in our discussion of the documented transfer dilemma.

Training Intervention

The training intervention itself also works to maximize training transfer by incorporating effective instructional methods and learning principles. Various learning and transfer theories should drive the design of the training in order to increase the odds of engaging all trainees and increasing their learning. Before skimming this section because of the term *theory*, please read on; these adult learning principles are crucial to incorporate when designing any training stimulus, whether it be formal or informal, on the job or off the job, and so on.

Adult learning theory. Specific elements of adult learning theory, which instructional design principles advocate, include the following (Knowles, 1990):

- People learn more when their "need to know" is high and their WIFM (what's in it for me) is crystal clear. They will then self-direct their learning.

- People learn best if they are exposed to the overall view of how all the training elements fit together, before delving into the specifics.

- People learn by hearing, seeing, and doing. Try to appeal to visual, audio, and tactile learners. Make training active, not passive, and cover the same information in different ways.

- People learn by observing and interacting with others. Learning is a social activity and therefore group, as well as individual, activities should be integrated into programs.

- People need to use their own life or work-related experience as a basis for learning. Trainees should bring actual work-relevant problems to training.

- People learn more when there is a "problem-centered" focus in training, in which they attempt to solve a problem that is relevant to their world.

- People need opportunities to practice. These practice sessions should occur frequently during training and after training, too.

- People need and will improve with immediate feedback. Trainers and co-trainees should target specific, behavioral comments in training practice sessions.

- People are motivated to learn by both extrinsic and intrinsic motivators. For example, incorporating training and development into merit increases can be motivating for trainees, as can the opportunity for trainees to feel personal accomplishment for demonstrating a new or refined skill.

Identical elements theory. Another design principle that should be incorporated into training interventions in order to enhance transfer is the theory of identical elements (Thorndike & Woodworth, 1901). Identical elements theory merely suggests that your training stimulus should mimic the job setting and job task as closely as possible. This theory also speaks to the need for "placing training as close to the job as possible." This means that if training can be done on the job, then trainers should do it. For example, if military personnel need to become proficient in self-aid and buddy care techniques, then trainers should design, develop, and deliver the training out on the flight line, using actual equipment and realistically simulated injuries, instead of plopping trainees down in front of some first-aid video clip and expecting them to learn!

Other relevant theories. Other learning theories should also inform program design in order to increase training transfer (see Noe, 1999 for a more comprehensive review). For example, specific, measurable learning objectives should be created for programs and for trainees' use of skills on the job. Credible, knowledgeable instructors should also be used at all times. One of the most tedious processes I engaged in when working in corporate training was selecting my in-house trainers. It was clear that these people would be viewed as the role models to emulate in certain workplace skills (such as effective business presentations) and that their role in the training intervention would be paramount. Therefore, only the cream of the crop was chosen. In addition, positive reinforcement should follow the demonstration of any favorable trainee response, question, or participation.

And finally, trainees need to believe they can learn the content and that it is valuable to their job performance. Why do firms continue to send employees to training that they don't need or to programs that they don't have the basic skills to perform? When I taught effective business presentations in the corporate environment, it was somewhat astonishing to me how many trainees showed up to programs either (a) unaware of why they were nominated to attend (some didn't even give presentations in their job) or (b) lacking in baseline oral communication skills. These situations are inexcusable and degrade the value of the training system. If such occurrences are happening in your firm, then action should be taken to improve trainee selection and communication of program goals and prerequisites to supervisors and employees.

Transfer Outcomes

Lastly, we come to the outcome-side of the model in figure 5.1. Here we see the evaluative transfer outcomes of (a) ability and motivation to transfer, (b) the use of transfer strategies, and most importantly, (c) behavioral change on the job. Motivation to transfer is simply the trainees' desire to use the trained knowledge and skills on their job. If a trainee intends to use the trained skills, he or she likely has a high motivation to apply training on the job. Ability to transfer is a recently conceived construct that refers to the degree to which trainees have the "tools" or skills needed to cope with work situations that threaten their skill maintenance (Burke, 1996). This concept is similar to (yet different from) self-efficacy, the more broadly substantiated construct that refers to a person's judgment of his or her ability to perform a given task (see, for example, Gist, Stevens, & Bavetta, 1991). Ability to transfer more specifically conveys the notion of whether a trainee is equipped with the skills necessary to help him use training back on the job.

The use of transfer strategies is the extent to which trainees utilize cognitive and behavioral tactics to apply the initial training to enhance their job performance. In the next section, useful transfer strategies that can be imparted to trainees during the initial training intervention are discussed.

And finally, behavioral change, which is arguably the most important out-come, refers to either of the following:

- maintenance, the retention of learned knowledge and skills on the job over time, or

- generalization, the extent to which trained skills are applied to different tasks or in other settings beyond those presented in the initial training.

In summary, figure 5.1 illustrates that training transfer is a product of pre- and post-influences, as well as, elements of program design. For those individuals responsible for organizational training, the model demon-strates that training transfer is embedded amongst many influences. Con-sequently, tackling transfer within an organization should follow a systemic, programmatic approach to address influences before, during, and after training. In the next section, the more effective transfer interven-tions, according to recent research, are outlined.

OTHER MEANS OF INCREASING TRANSFER

Aside from integrating adult learning principles into training, the meth-ods organizations can use to increase transfer basically fall into two catego-ries (Bennett, Lehman, & Forst, 1999): (a) transfer climate interventions that target the larger performance management system in the firm, and/or (b) posttraining transfer interventions (such as relapse prevention training). Given what we have discussed so far, it is highly likely that an organization may have to consider a holistic approach, that is, to pursue some element of both types of interventions in order to have a marked effect on transfer. Transfer climate is surely one of the more critical variables in the mix, but some type of instructed coping skills during the training intervention may also be needed, at least in hostile transfer climates. To illustrate this asser-tion, in this section the highlights are shared from a study in one large cor-poration of a posttraining intervention, called relapse prevention, and transfer climate.

Relapse Prevention (RP) and Transfer Climate

To investigate fruitful ways to bolster training transfer, the posttraining transfer intervention, relapse prevention (RP), and perceived transfer cli-mate were investigated in a large Midwestern firm. This was the first time RP had ever been tested in an actual corporate training setting. Nonethe-less, a great deal of conceptual support existed in the literature as to the con-ceptually and intuitively appealing nature of RP as a transfer intervention (Marx, 1982).

There were seventy-eight research scientists who participated in the study. The scientists were all supervisors who initially attended a training program to enhance their employee coaching skills. Specifically, the coaching program addressed the role of coaching in supervising employees, examined opportunities for coaching, identified ways coaching would make a supervisor's job easier, and developed and provided practice opportunities (for example, providing feedback). Two different RP modules were administered after the coaching modules (posttraining) to various trainees, while other participants were in a control group that received the coaching module, but not RP.

The first RP module tested was essentially a full-blown version as originally proposed by Bob Marx (1982). In other words, it contained all of the RP techniques as outlined in appendices 5A, 5B, and 5C. The second RP module, however, was a scaled-down version that only had a couple elements of RP in order to see if a more efficient method was effective. The elements included in the scaled-down version were selected based upon findings in prior research of what appeared to be the more effective components of RP (for example, self-monitoring).

Background on RP. Relapse prevention originated in the clinical psychology arena (Marlatt & Gordon, 1985), specifically designed to enhance the maintenance stage in the treatment of addictive behaviors (smoking, alcohol, and drug cessation programs). Based on self-management principles, RP attempts to teach individuals how to actively anticipate and cope with a relapse into former habitual behaviors. In this way, RP acknowledges the work environment's influence on a trainee's ability to maintain learned skills and suggests that trainees should be provided coping skills to deal with it.

Specifically, RP training combines behavioral skills with cognitive self-management strategies to make trainees aware of environmental and intrapersonal threats to skill maintenance. These threats are referred to as high-risk situations, which threaten the employee's sense of control and increase the risk of their eventual relapse (Marx, 1982). As such, a relapse occurs at the intersection of a high-risk situation and a coping skill deficit. By identifying trainees' high-risk situations and developing appropriate coping skills in RP training, trainees can anticipate and ultimately prevent relapse, as well as recover from a temporary lapse if it occurs.

There are several examples of commonly experienced high-risk situations that can threaten a trainee's training transfer (Marx, 1986a, 1986b). Potential intrapersonal high-risk situations may include the following:

- employee stress
- negative mood state
- lack of career motivation
- lack of job motivation

- absence of necessary support skills (for example, time management, listening)
- disruptive events in a trainee's personal life

And high-risk situations that emanate from a trainee's work environment are considered to include these factors:

- time pressures and deadlines
- work overload and crises
- lack of necessary tools, equipment, and resources
- lack of support from coworkers or boss
- lack of opportunities to apply trained skills
- the presence of interpersonal work conflicts

Reflect upon a simple example in the corporate training setting from the study in question. In a training module designed to enhance supervisors' coaching skills, supervisors will likely return to work only to find numerous critical deadlines and work pressures. The immediate gratification for completing their own tasks (especially for these research scientists who prefer autonomous work environments), instead of taking time to coach their subordinates, may cause the supervisors to lapse into old behavior (that is, not coach or do so poorly). Consequently, a high-risk situation, such as work pressures, has threatened the supervisor's use of new coaching skills, and as a result he may miss opportunities to coach, blame himself for not trying harder to coach, lose confidence in his ability to coach, and as a result, eventually relapse.

So what do trainees do in RP training? In addition to valuable goal-setting and self-monitoring components, RP training includes fourteen specific strategies that help trainees (1) anticipate and monitor potential difficulties affecting transfer, (2) diagnose related support skills, (3) increase their rational thinking, and (4) identify appropriate consequences for transfer-related behavior (Marx, 1982). Appendices 5A, 5B, and 5C contain specific illustrations of handouts used with these research scientists to implement Marx's proposed approach.

Appendix 5A is a training handout that can be used by practitioners as a worksheet to guide participants through an RP posttraining intervention. It is important to note that trainees might need extra guidance on steps 1 and 2, so trainers should be prepared to provide *relevant* examples of skill maintenance goals and slips.

Appendix 5B is a description of each of the fourteen specific RP cognitive and behavioral coping skills. It can be used during an RP training program and, more importantly, as a follow-up job aid to help trainees remember the strategies. It is written in clear terms and should be customized based upon the nature of the initial training program (that is, certain strategies could be modified or deleted if not applicable to the initial training).

Appendix 5C is a self-monitoring record that employees can use to track their skill maintenance after training. Trainees keep the sheet visible in their workspace and track their transfer by using a simple coding scheme. The scheme includes notation to indicate successful maintenance, a temporary lapse, and total relapse back into old habits.

Relevant findings. The results of this study revealed several points of importance to trainers. First, a supportive individual transfer climate significantly increased the trainees' use of transfer strategies back on the job. Second, the full-blown RP training enhanced maintenance outcomes in unfavorable transfer climates, whereas the scaled-down version of RP training enhanced maintenance outcomes in favorable transfer climates. Lastly, ability and motivation to transfer partially accounted for the relationship between individual transfer climate and the trainees' use of transfer strategies (Burke, 1996). Each finding is discussed in turn.

The first finding is extremely consistent with recent empirical work on the critical influence of transfer climate. It tells us that the trainees' work context will be largely responsible for their motivation and performance in a training program and ultimate use of training on the job. Regarding the second finding, the scaled-down RP module interacted with transfer climate differently than the full RP module, across all the training outcomes that were measured. These outcome variables included a self-report number of coaching sessions, a subordinate measure of supervisory coaching effectiveness, and a self-report measure of transfer strategy use. More specifically, the full RP module significantly produced the greatest influence on transfer in the least supportive climates, while the modified RP (and control) group tended to produce greater transfer rates in the more supportive climates. What is more important is the fact that had transfer climate not been simultaneously explored in the study, the findings would have been distorted, misleading, and oversimplified. Instead, by incorporating the measurement of transfer climate, the study verified the importance of contextual factors, and how they impact the need for, and design of, posttraining interventions.

Finally, there was evidence that ability and motivation to transfer are important factors that help to account for the effect of transfer climate on transfer outcomes. Hence, both of these variables deserve our attention in the design of posttraining interventions. And ability to transfer should be incorporated in future transfer studies.

Other qualitative data were also collected. Trainees in the full-blown RP condition were asked how useful they considered each component in this transfer intervention. Accordingly, 67 percent reported the goal-setting component to be useful (step 2 in appendix 5A); a small 33 percent agreed the decision matrix was useful (step 3); 67 percent thought it was helpful to predict their first slip (step 5); one-half of trainees claimed that it was beneficial to generate coping skills to enhance their transfer (step 6); and finally, 80 percent found the self-monitoring tool to be useful (step 7) (Burke, 1996). Given this data, we see that a job aid can be a very helpful device for supporting training transfer.

Implications for practice. Based on the aforementioned trainee feedback and the previously discussed interaction findings between RP and transfer climate, several practical suggestions can be advanced for trainers. These suggestions regarding the use of RP are depicted in table 5.1.

As illustrated, the two proposed RP modules are designed to accommodate different transfer climates—favorable and unfavorable climates. Trainees in favorable transfer climates appear to benefit more from efficient transfer interventions that incorporate a few simple but useful coping strategies and skills addressing common relapse antecedents (for example, time pressure, work overload). Yet, such a simple arsenal of skills is likely insufficient to battle relapse challenges in an unfavorable climate, where self-management tools are quintessential to combat work environment, interpersonal, and intrapersonal transfer threats (Burke & Baldwin, 1999). Therefore, it could be disastrous to just start using RP interventions at the end of all your initial training programs; some thoughtful efforts and strategizing are needed to ensure that the most appropriate tools are used in the most appropriate situations.

It should also be noted that the specific RP modules in table 5.1 are somewhat different from Marx's proposal. Based on trainee feedback, the decision matrix component (step 3 in appendix 5A) was eliminated. Also, it appears that the use of the fourteen specific RP strategies (step 4 in appendix 5A) should actually be determined by the initial training module content and the nature of the climate that trainees face.

But before RP can be implemented in an organization, trainers must first address several issues to determine if RP is conceptually appropriate for their initial program and situation. If the answer to these four questions is "yes," RP is likely to be more appropriate and effective.

1. Are there tangible skills trainees learn in the initial training program that they are expected to demonstrate and maintain back on the job?
2. Are trainees tempted to relapse into old behaviors due to immediate gratification of old habits?
3. Are there various high-risk situations trainees face on the job that threaten the use of their newly trained skills?
4. Are trainees ready for and committed to behavioral change and do they view the training as a priority in their everyday work?

These four questions stress the importance of trainers having an accurate conception of what RP is all about, its fundamental premise and philos-

Table 5.1
Recommendations for Relapse Prevention Training Modules (Based on Type of Transfer Climate)

RP Module for Hostile Transfer Climates	RP Module for Favorable Transfer Climates
Step 1. State the skill to maintain	Step 1. RP strategies[1]
Step 2. Define goal, slip, relapse	Step 2. Predict the first slip
Step 3. RP strategies[1]	Step 3. Generate coping skills
Step 4. Predict the first slip	Step 4. Self-monitoring on the job
Step 5. Generate coping skills	
Step 6. Self-monitoring on the job	

[1] Strategy selection should be determined by intial program content and the type of transfer climate trainees face.

Adapted from: L.A. Burke, Improving transfer of training: A field investigation of the effect of relapse prevention training and transfer climate on maintenance outcomes (1996), *Dissertation Abstracts International*, 57-04A, 1725.

ophy, and its potential generalizability across various training interventions. As we can see, RP is (a) designed to target skill-based training (versus knowledge-based or attitudinal programs), (b) most appropriate when high-risk situations and instant gratification of habitual behaviors is apparent, and (c) most effective when trainees really want to change their workplace behaviors.

In summary, RP training appears to be an effective transfer intervention only when we use it appropriately and in the right situations. As we might have suspected, a full-blown RP module tends to works best in hostile transfer climates. Consequently, trainers should assess their trainees' perceived transfer climate and, if conceptually appropriate, invoke an RP intervention that is congruent with the type of transfer climate trainees face. As illustrated in table 5.1, there is less need for an extensive posttraining transfer intervention in more favorable transfer environments. In these instances, initially attacking the transfer climate may be the most appropriate long-term strategy.

Finally, one important caveat should be reiterated. We as training professionals cannot be seduced into thinking that posttraining interventions will, on their own, provide a quick, complete, or easy fix to the transfer problem. Certainly, we cannot just plop a transfer intervention at the end of every program in our organization and expect immediate results. A holistic and systematic approach, which considers the nature of the transfer climate, is necessary. And a trainee's total work situation including immediate supervisory support, attitudes of others, and training policies and practices should help to determine the need for, as well as the design of, posttraining interventions. In sum, the transfer problem is likely to (a) be stubbornly entrenched and context-dependent and (b) require a long-term solution using methodical assessment and action.

TRANSFER ACTION PLANS FOR HIGH IMPACT

So, where do we go from here? That is, from a broader perspective, how can we make sense of all the existing information in the literature and across various studies in order to offer specific recommendations for increasing transfer rates? In this section, a plethora of practical recommendations (above and beyond those already mentioned) is compiled into a simplified, yet meaningful, framework. The framework is based upon the three stages of time relevant to a training intervention (before, during, after) and the key players involved (trainer, trainee, and supervisor). These elements all represent critical components of a transfer-enhancement action plan (Wexley & Latham, 1991).

Trainer's Transfer Enhancement Plan

First, let's examine a trainer's responsibilities across these three stages of training. In table 5.2, there are specific actions to highlight so trainers can ensure maximum transfer. Their role is not merely limited to what transpires during the training program. Indeed, trainers have more opportunity to rectify the transfer problem than what some might initially think. The appropriate level of transfer responsibility for trainers is depicted in table 5.2.

Some individuals believe trainers need to just "train right" and then leave the rest of the transfer responsibility to the trainees. Nothing could be more wrong! Trainers can and should play a much more active role in the pre- and posttraining stages.

In terms of the pretraining stage, trainers need to ensure that the training system is operating as it should: needs assessment, creation of appropriate learning objectives, effective program design and development, and follow-up program evaluation. Trainers can also increase transfer by setting the stage with supervisors and trainees before the intervention so that the appropriate supervisor-trainee discussions are occurring and so that trainees come adequately prepared to the program.

What appears to be the biggest opportunity for improvement, however, is trainer involvement in the posttraining phase. It is at this time where trainers can facilitate on-going transfer support mechanisms for trainees such as peer support networks, field visits, continual improvement, and so

Table 5.2
Trainer's Transfer Enhancement Plan

Pretraining	During Training	Posttraining
• Ensure appropriate needs assessment	• Create a nurturing setting; make "WIIFM" clear	• Facilitate peer support forums to discuss posttraining experiences and to reinforce coping skills
• Ensure training ties to business strategy	• Employ adult learning principles and encourage active trainee participation	• Remind trainees and supervisors of the initial training objectives
• Measure transfer climate to determine appropriate transfer intervention	• Teach mnemonic devices that are helpful in transfer	• Send copy of trainees' action plans to them one month posttraining, along with transfer-enhancing job aids
• Send welcome notification to employees, creating anticipation	• Test for retention periodically	• Conduct field visits to observe skill use and solicit feedback to improve training's transfer potential
• Communicate to trainees and their supervisors the "WIIFM," training objectives, and importance of transfer	• Provide trainees with appropriate self-management skills to maintain training	• Evaluate training: conduct follow-up measurement to ascertain degree of trainee transfer
• Encourage managers to discuss application ideas and expectations with trainees	• Ensure trainees set application goals (e.g., action planning)	• Make recommended changes towards spirit of improving
• Ask trainees to bring relevant work problems and issues to the training	• Facilitate creation of peer networks for trainee posttraining support	
• Design training to support transfer	• Provide trainer contact information for trainee follow-up	

on. It is my experience that this is the stage where most trainers unfortunately fade out of the picture.

Trainee's Transfer Enhancement Plan

Next, let's examine the trainees' role in ensuring that the knowledge, skills, and abilities they receive in training are actually used back on the job. Table 5.3 represents the trainee's transfer game plan.

As detailed in this exhibit, trainees should not be expected merely "to show up to the program." If trainees come to a program and have absolutely no clue why they have been nominated to attend, the trainer should

Table 5.3
Trainee's Transfer Enhancement Plan

Pretraining	During Training	Posttraining
• Clearly understand training goals	• Focus and actively participate	• Discuss learning and action plan with supervisor
• Discuss training objectives and expectations with supervisor to apply learning	• Establish specific, measurable, realistic goals for using the trained skills (i.e., action planning)	• Meet with support network and discuss transfer challenges, personal progress, best practices in transfer (e.g., self-monitoring)
• Articulate a "WIIFM"	• Identify peer network and other resources for ongoing support of skill application	
• Take specific work relevant problems to the training and seek solutions		• Use the trained skills on the job
• Discuss potential challenges that threaten transfer in work setting with supervisor, and identify specific methods for dealing with them	• Prepare for slipping back into old behavioral patterns in high-risk situations	• Practice self-management coping skill techniques (e.g., identify high-risk situations and coping skills to deal with them)
• Hand off important job tasks to someone else while at training	• Discuss self-management strategies to enhance transfer and exchange examples of how such strategies can be used at work	• Provide trainer with feedback regarding transfer
		• Share trained skill and knowledge with others

send them back to work and then follow up with their supervisor. It's simply unacceptable for this to happen.

In contrast, to increase transfer, trainees need to be actively engaged and managing their skill application before, during, and after the intervention. The more frequent tasks for trainees in table 5.3 cluster around one action item—interaction with their supervisor to facilitate the appropriate "transfer conversations." There is also the theme of self-management that is apparent in that trainees take an active role in managing themselves and their work environment, as needed, to increase skill maintenance. Moreover, we see that trainees should be held responsible for learning and applying coping skills that can decrease their chance of relapsing into bad habits.

Supervisor's Transfer Enhancement Plan

Lastly, what should supervisors of trainees be doing to enhance transfer rates? Clearly, supervisors have a vested interest in transfer to make sure that employees are appropriately progressing and developing on the job and making good use of the training they are nominated to attend. In other words, the organization's supervisory personnel need to be focused on increasing their return on investment from training. Table 5.4 illustrates first-line supervisors' responsibilities.

Table 5.4 illustrates that supervisors cannot merely nominate employees to attend whatever training programs are available and then let nature take its course. Unfortunately, this happens all too often. Instead, line supervisors must be actively involved in employee development, including identifying specific training needs, initiating appropriate transfer discussions before and after training, and taking note of subordinates who successfully transfer (as well as those who don't).

What is so painfully obvious to most trainers (but perhaps not to supervisors) is that line managers model their personal support of training in numerous ways—directly and indirectly via what they say and do, and by

Table 5.4
Supervisor's Transfer Enhancement Plan

Pretraining	During Training	Posttraining
• Support training department and the development of business-relevant training	• Reassign trainee's workload during training	• Coach the employee
• Identify and select employees for whom training is relevant, necessary, and valuable	• Ensure employee is not interrupted during the training, unless critical	• Have employee share learning with colleagues
• Meet with employees to discuss their personal development plan, role of training they attend, and goals	• Ask employees to relay feedback during program, as appropriate.	• Provide opportunities for employee to apply training
• Communicate training importance and discuss application ideas and expectations	• Offer to speak during the training about its importance or to lead as a trainer, if appropriate	• Provide timely feedback and recognition when employee uses new skills.
• Discuss trainee's "WIIFM"	• Visit the session or attend a luncheon during training to show support	• Create a positive work environment for transfer
		• Discuss the use of transfer coping skills with employee
		• Inform trainer/external consultant of application results and demand continual improvement

what they think, believe, and feel. In other words, supervisors cannot just superficially support training and development when convenient or just as an afterthought. It needs to be an on-going commitment felt in their heart and modeled in their actions. The corporate culture and genuine top management support facilitate such feelings and demonstrations of commitment.

Research has shown that one of the most important and vital supervisory activities to support transfer is coaching (Morano & Deets, 1986; Robinson & Robinson, 1989). In fact, some research suggests that the absence of coaching can account for up to 80 percent of the loss in training investment (Robinson & Robinson, 1989). Coaching refers not only to the reinforcement of trainees' use of trained skills on the job, but also to the conversations supervisors have with employees immediately after training and before they attempt to use the skills.

For example, if an employee returns from a conflict management skills workshop, a supervisor should sit down with that employee and discuss the learned skills, opportunities for applications, and specific pointers on applying the skills in his/her particular job function. After demonstrating the conflict management skills in action, the supervisor should then provide meaningful feedback. Based on learning frameworks used at Xerox (Fox, 1983), supervisors should realize that coaching is not equivalent with cheerleading, it is not a one-time occurrence, and it does not mean that supervisors "take over" situations. To coach, supervisors must learn to meaningfully observe employee behavior, to continually provide specific, behavioral feedback, and to identify problems.

Furthermore, line managers should work to "close the loop" by following up with trainers after a program (especially with external consultants) and providing feedback with the intent of continually improving a program's transfer potential. Managers who do not diligently monitor program results and communicate these results back to trainers are pursuing low-impact methods.

To sum up, in this section we have outlined various specific recommendations that trainers, trainees, and supervisors can use to increase transfer rates. We have learned that the traditional roles assigned to these three key parties—that "supervisors nominate," "trainees attend," and "trainers train"—is simply not enough to address such an entrenched training problem. The critical take-away for practitioners is that in order to reap the benefit of your training programs, everyone involved must get serious, become actively engaged, and make the transfer climate more favorable.

MEASURING TRANSFER RATES

In addition to tools, methods, and techniques for improving transfer, trainers may want to measure transfer rates across the programs they offer. In their Waste Isolation Division, Westinghouse Electric Corporation developed a valuable, relevant, and practical transfer evaluation model under contract with the Department of Energy (Carlsbad Area Office). Their transfer evaluation model is referred to as TOTEM—the transfer of training evaluation model. TOTEM measures the transfer of training rate from the classroom to the job through fairly simple, anonymous posttraining surveys of trainees. Upon completing a technology transfer document, trainers can obtain nonexclusive rights to this model and adopt it for their own organizational use (see http://www.t2ed.com).

In developing TOTEM, the creators set out to develop a transfer measurement model that was cost- and user-friendly. Their originally stated criteria, which should satisfy—or exceed—most trainers' needs, included (TOTEM: Transfer of Training Model, 1995, p. 6):

- Provide an overall transfer rate for any given course.

- Provide transfer of training rates for all major content areas of any given course.

- Provide instructional staff with clear, concise feedback for systematically improving transfer, including (1) content areas that need more instruction, (2) content areas that need less instruction, and 3) content areas that should be left alone.

- Be user (instructional staff, administrative staff, and management) friendly—easy to use and interpret, and readily computerized.

- Be inexpensive to use.

- Ensure valid results by (1) determining if the trainees possessed the skills and knowledge before taking the class, (2) minimizing defensive and socially desirable trainee responses and (3) maximizing honest feedback.

By meeting these criteria, TOTEM measures transfer simply and efficiently. Although not absent limitations, this measurement model provides practitioners with a prescribed method for calculating transfer rates in a training program, thereby quantifying trainees' transfer behaviors. Ultimately, the use of such models will feed useful data to managers and instructors and can be used to continually improve an organization's training efforts.

FINAL THOUGHTS

In this chapter, the challenging issue of training transfer was addressed, including reasons why the transfer problem often gets ignored in organizations, various factors that influence transfer, and finally, some of the more successful and effective transfer interventions. Specifically, we examined relapse prevention training as a posttraining transfer intervention and its interaction with the important contextual variable of transfer climate. A simplified framework was then advanced for tackling the documented transfer dilemma, which outlined specific practical actions that trainers, trainees, and managers can take (before, during, and after programs) to effectively increase the extent to which trainees use training back at work. Finally, a specific model for measuring transfer rates was presented. Indeed, training professionals need to continually refine and hone the so-phistication of their training system and work to maximize the outcomes pursued.

From a broader perspective, all human resource subsystems (recruiting, selection, compensation, and performance management), practices, and personnel within the organization should be poised to support training transfer. If not, organizations will likely experience disappointing rates of actual trained skill usage. Therefore, human resource professionals must view training transfer as integrally related to the larger spectrum of organizational practices (Burke, 1996).

Specifically, practitioners should attempt to recruit and select persons who are highly motivated and capable of acquiring new knowledge and skills, who are able to manage themselves on the job, and who hold themselves accountable for performance improvement. Managers should actively hold trainees accountable and publicly reward them for transferring newly learned skills and behaviors to their job. This dictates that the maintenance of learned skills be included in performance appraisals in order to provide feedback. And company efforts to improve training transfer should be linked to priority performance improvement needs and integral to top management goals.

Given the importance and increasing dominance of a "learning mindset" in the current competitive climate, training professionals need to be striving for maximizing the effects of their training interventions. As such, integral to high-impact training is ensuring that trainees are actually using their trained knowledge and skills at work, sharing their learning with others, and taking their personal development within the organization seriously. Without these outcomes, training becomes an unnecessary appendage that stalls employee and organizational development.

So once again, trainers are confronted with a challenge to tackle head on. Use the information in this chapter to examine in your firm the various influences on transfer such as your trainees' characteristics, the design of your programs, the use of appropriate learning and transfer principles and practices, and the nature of your trainees' transfer climate. Measure not only trainees' reactions to programs, but also the degree of their learning and behavioral changes back on the job—whether by surveys, interviews, or observations. Consider the most appropriate interventions and techniques for combating your organization's transfer problem including posttraining transfer interventions (such as relapse prevention), transfer climate interventions, and/or transfer-enhancement action plans for trainees, trainers, and supervisors.

BIBLIOGRAPHY

Baldwin, T.T., & Ford, J.K. (1988). Transfer of training: A review and directions for future research. *Personnel Psychology, 41,* 63–106.

Barrick, M.R., Mount, M.K., & Strauss, J.P. (1993). Conscientiousness and performance on sales representatives: Test of the mediating effects of goal setting. *Journal of Applied Psychology, 78,* 715–722.

Bennett, J.B., Lehman, W.E.K., & Forst, J.K. (1999). Change, transfer climate, and customer orientation: A contextual model and analysis of change-driven training. *Group and Organization Management, 24,* 188–216.

Burke, L.A. (1996). Improving transfer of training: A field investigation of the effect of relapse prevention training and transfer climate on maintenance outcomes. *Dissertation Abstracts International, 57-04A,* 1725. Accession no: AAG9627025.

Burke, L.A., & Baldwin, T.T. (1999). Workforce training transfer: A study of the effect of relapse prevention training and transfer climate. *Human Resource Management, 38,* 227–242.

Fox, D. (1983). Coaching: The way to protect your sales training investment. *Training and Development Journal, 37(11),* 37–40.

Gist, M.E., Stevens, C.K., & Bavetta, A.G. (1991). Effects of self-efficacy and posttraining interventions on the acquisition and maintenance of complex interpersonal skills. *Personnel Psychology, 44,* 837–861.

Knowles, M. (1990). *The adult learner* (4th ed.). Houston: Gulf Publishing.

Marlatt, G.A., & Gordon, J.R. (Eds.). (1985). *Relapse prevention: Maintaining strategies in the treatment of addictive behaviors.* New York: Guilford Publications.

Marx, R.D. (1982). Relapse prevention for managerial training: A model for maintenance of behavioral change. *Academy of Management Review, 7,* 433–441.

Marx, R.D. (1986a). Self-managed skill retention. *Training and Development Journal, 40,* 54–57.

Marx, R.D. (1986). Improving management development through relapse prevention strategies, *Journal of Management Development, 5,* 27–40.

Morano, R.A., & Deets, N. (1986). Keeping technologists on the road to the future. *Training and Development Journal, 40(12),* 38–42.

Mount, M.K., & Barrick, M.R. (1995). The big five personality dimensions: Implications for research and practice in human resources management. In G.R. Ferris (Ed.). *Research in Personnel and Human Resources Management* (pp. 153–200). Greenwich, CT: JAI Press.

Newstrom, J.W. (1986). Leveraging management development through the management of transfer. *Journal of Management Development, 5,* 33–45.

Noe, R.A. (1999). *Employee training & development.* Boston: Irwin McGraw-Hill.

Robinson, D.G., & Robinson, J. (1989). *Training for impact: How to link training to business needs and measure the results.* San Francisco: Jossey-Bass.

Rouiller, J.Z., & Goldstein, I.L. (1993). The relationship between organizational transfer climate and positive transfer of training. *Human Resource Development Quarterly, 4,* 377–390.

Tannenbaum, S.I., Cannon-Bowers, J.A., Salas, E., & Mathieu, J.E. (1993). *Factors that influence training effectiveness: A conceptual model and longitudinal analysis.* (NAWCTSD Technical Report 93-011). Orlando, FL: Naval Air Warfare Center.

Thorndike, E.L., & Woodworth, R.S. (1901). The influence of improvement of one mental function upon the efficiency of other functions. *Psychological Review, 8,* 247–261.

TOTEM: Transfer of training evaluation model. (1995). Waste Isolation Division: Westinghouse Electric Corporation. Carlsbad, NM: Department of Energy.

Tyler, K. (2000, May). Hold on to what you've learned. *HR Magazine*, 94–102.

Wexley, K.N., & Latham, G.P. (1991). *Developing and training human resources in organizations* (2nd ed.). New York: HarperCollins.

APPENDIX 5A: RELAPSE PREVENTION TRAINING AID

Step 1. State the trained skill you wish to apply and maintain from this training.

Step 2. Set your skill maintenance goal, based upon this training.

Set a specific, measurable, short-range goal. Then, specifically define a slip and a relapse.

Skill Maintenance Goal: _____

Slip: _____

Relapse: _____

Step 3. Understand positive and negative consequences of using the skill at work.

Positive Consequences of Using Your New Skills: _____

Negative Consequences of Not Using Your New Skills: _____

Positive Consequences of Not Using Your New Skills: _____

Negative Consequences of Using Your New Skills: _____

Step 4. Apply the relapse prevention strategies to maintain trained skills.

RP Strategy	Trainee Notes/Comments
1. Understand the relapse process (i.e., slip, then relapse).	
2. Understand the difference between the training and job contexts.	
3. Create a support network.	
4. Be aware of subordinate skepticism of new skills.	
5. Identify high-risk situations.	
6. Apply skills in the appropriate setting.	
7. Understand seemingly unimportant behaviors that may lead to a relapse.	
8. Reduce interfering and unproductive emotions.	
9. Retain your self-confidence, despite slips.	
10. Diagnose support skills needed to maintain training.	
11. Review disruptive lifestyle patterns.	
12. Mix enjoyable and tedious work tasks.	

13. Diagnose support back at work for skill application.

14. Create meaningful self-rewards for skill retention.

Step 5. Describe the nature of circumstances that will likely surround a first slip.

Step 6. Generate ideas for how you will deal with such difficult situations.

Step 7. Monitor your behavior at work with the self-monitoring record (see Appendix 5B).

Adapted from: Burke, L.A. (1996). Improving transfer of training: A field investigation of the effect of relapse prevention training and transfer climate on maintenance outcomes. *Dissertation Abstracts International*, 57-04A, 1725.

APPENDIX 5B: RELAPSE PREVENTION STRATEGIES—TRAINEES' GUIDE FOR FUTURE REFERENCE

1. Understand the relapse process.

After learning new skills in training programs, you will likely encounter high-risk situations that threaten the use of your skills back on the job. It is therefore important to have a plan for coping with high-risk situations in order to decrease the probability of relapse (i.e., reverting to former behaviors/habits).

2. Note the training/job difference.

Training programs present very safe environments for trainees to experiment with and discuss the use of new skills. However, often the work environment trainees return to is less supportive for applying the new skills. You should be aware of this difference and be prepared to deal with it.

3. Create a support network.

After leaving a program, try to maintain contact with other trainees in order to exchange your experiences and ideas for using the new skills back at work. This support network can be very useful in obtaining advice and ideas for dealing with situations you encounter on the job. It also allows you the opportunity to recognize your successes in using the new skill.

4. Be aware of subordinate skepticism.

Sometimes subordinates are skeptical of new behaviors that supervisors exhibit on the job. You should educate your employees about the training programs you attend and the new techniques you employ on the job to lessen their skepticism. In addition, making a gradual transition to the use of new skills, instead of an abrupt change, may help to avoid subordinate skepticism.

5. Identify high-risk situations.

High-risk situations are environmental or intrapersonal threats to your use of newly trained skills. It is critical that you understand and identify the specific high-risk situations you will likely face in applying trained skills and have a plan for how you will cope with the high-risk situations.

6. Use in the appropriate setting.

You should implement new skills in the appropriate situation or setting. For example, from a coaching module, trainees should understand the appropriate timing for giving feedback or the difference between coaching and counseling. In doing so, trainees can increase their chances of successfully using the coaching skills.

7. Be aware of seemingly unimportant behaviors that lead to error.

Seemingly unimportant behaviors that lead to error (SUBTLE) refers to times in which you engage in behaviors that ultimately threaten your use of the newly acquired skills. For example, in a coaching module, a trainee may decide that setting up one-on-one sessions with subordinates would be beneficial, but proceed to set up meetings at a time in which they will likely be canceled. It is important that trainees do not set themselves up to fail at using the new skill.

8. Reduce interfering emotions.

Some emotional reactions may interfere with your learning and continued application of skills (e.g., getting upset, feeling guilty). You should try to decrease the occurrence of such emotions when attempting to use newly learned skills.

9. Retain self-confidence despite slips.

It is important that you retain your self-confidence when using new skills, especially when you slip into old behavior. Slips should be viewed as temporary, expected occurrences from which to learn. You should not view a slip as a personal failure.

10. Diagnose other support skills.

Often it is important to possess other skills when applying the specific skill you have learned. For example, to effectively use coaching skills, trainees should be able to listen actively, motivate and influence others, and manage their time well—all are important support skills for coaching.

11. Review disruptive lifestyle patterns.

Trainees may have certain lifestyle patterns or habits that get in the way of using the newly acquired skills. For example, perfectionism can cause trainees to be unduly critical of their early attempts in using new skills or cause trainees to avoid using the skill so they won't make a "mistake." Also, resistance to change can interfere with trying to use new skills.

12. Mix enjoyable and tedious tasks.

It is important to mix desirable and tedious work activities. In doing so, using new skills can be facilitated since you are not overwhelmed by unenjoyable tasks.

13. Diagnose support back at work.

The support of subordinates, peers, and supervisors is important when using new skills back on the job. You should diagnose how supportive your work environment is and make attempts to enlist support (e.g., increase awareness, educate others).

14. *Create meaningful self-rewards.*

Research has shown that employees tend to punish themselves more often than reward themselves at work. Therefore, whenever you succeed in using a new skill on the job, you should praise yourself (i.e., give yourself a pat on the back) and/or create other self-rewards that are meaningful to you.

Adapted from: Burke, L.A. (1996). Improving transfer of training: A field investigation of the effect of relapse prevention training and transfer climate on maintenance outcomes. *Dissertation Abstracts International,* 57-04A, 1725.

APPENDIX 5C: SELF-MONITORING RECORD

Please keep this record where you will see it on a daily basis at work.

My skill maintenance goal: _____

Slip: _____

Relapse: _____

Please indicate in the boxes whether you have maintained your goal (X), slipped (S), or totally relapsed (R). Depending on your goal, you may want to track your progress at the end of every day and/or every week. Space is also provided to record comments regarding your feelings and thoughts.

Week of: _____   Comments:

Monday	Tuesday	Wednesday	Thursday	Friday

Week of: _____   Comments:

Monday	Tuesday	Wednesday	Thursday	Friday

Week of: _____   Comments:

Monday	Tuesday	Wednesday	Thursday	Friday

Adapted from: Burke, L.A. (1996). Improving transfer of training: A field investigation of the effect of relapse prevention training and transfer climate on maintenance outcomes. *Dissertation Abstracts International,* 57-04A, 1725.

Chapter 6

HOLISTIC TRAINING AND DEVELOPMENT: BEYOND CLASSROOM SOLUTIONS

L. Michael Wykes

In most organizations, learning in training interventions is often not transferred to the job. Consequently, the need exists to focus on factors in the workplace—the environment and support mechanisms—that may account for poor transfer. This need, in turn, drives trainers and human resource development (HRD) professionals toward a much broader role of resolving issues and removing performance inhibitors in an effort to integrate nontraining solutions for modifying employee behavior (Phillips, 2000). The emphasis is ultimately on improving organizational and departmental performance in the most efficient, yet effective, way possible.

The only way to assure that this corporately valued performance increase happens is through a holistic approach to solving employee performance issues. The necessity to meet executives' needs for business improvement dictates approaches that integrate a variety of different issues, techniques, and elements to bring about effective improvements—and affect the bottom line (that is, a return on investment that business leaders need) (Phillips, 1998). This integrated approach can take a number of different forms, but often the most effective form is that of performance consulting or human performance technology (HPT).

In sum, training professionals today are increasingly being asked to perform a broader role to help organizations achieve objectives. Instead of merely developing and delivering "programs," trainers are frequently asked to function as performance consultants. To perform these broader roles, training professionals have to think and act systemically. They have to be able to see the big picture, to figure out what is preventing top performance, and to help business leaders enhance performance in the most effective and efficient ways possible.

This chapter discusses the growing need for a performance focus, including the drivers behind this need and the reasons why trainers must adapt to this newer perspective. The origins of human performance technology are discussed, and a definition of the performance consultant's job is provided as well as the competence areas necessary to be successful. A simplified framework, which can help assure a systemic approach to performance, is presented. This framework uses concepts and tools from several leading proponents of performance consulting and human performance improvement. Finally, specific suggestions for beginning to focus on performance are also presented.

TRAINING: A COSTLY ISSUE

The financial implication of training is a big deal. Right now, the general training investment cost/benefit ratio appears to be upside down. According to the *Training Magazine* Industry Report 2000, large companies budgeted over 54 billion dollars in 1999 for a variety of training interventions (*Training*, 2000). The actual cost is probably much higher because this figure does not include training that occurs on a more informal basis or in small companies. This figure also excludes the enormous hidden expense of employee training, including the salaries employees are paid while they are engaged in training instead of working at their jobs. This translates into a huge investment by employers.

Even simple math highlights the huge implications. If we were to assume that training programs were able to transfer 20 percent of their yield into corporately valued outputs (admittedly a bit generous), that still means that over 43 billion dollars is spent each year on training program and interventions that may or may not affect business metrics. This presents a dismal cost/benefit ratio (as similarly voiced in chapter 5).

A systemic performance improvement approach, in the form of holistic performance consulting, offers a much greater potential to improve the cost/benefit ratio. At the very least, this holistic approach provides a solution mix to address key factors, rather than relying on just one type of intervention to carry a load it was not designed to carry.

TRAINING AND DEVELOPMENT PROFESSIONALS MUST ADAPT

The constant pressure for organizations and managers to adapt is not going to slow down in the foreseeable future. This realization produces many exciting possibilities, but it also presents a relative dark side concerning growth and survival. Trainers and others within specific corporate functions must figure out ways to meet changing needs quickly and efficiently, or run the risk of decreasing efficacy. Put simply, it is an "adapt or die" scenario.

The railroad industry provides a good example of this idea. Hardly anybody would contest the fact that railroads today are viewed primarily as utilitarian tools, mostly freight carriers, with limited passenger capabilities. This industry was the "king" when customer needs were relatively simple. They were the best—and only—game in town. Today, the industry is largely nondiversified and heavily subsidized. It is not really "dead," but it is not exactly an up-and-coming industry either.

Why? Railroad executives viewed themselves as being in the "railroad" business, not in the "transportation" business. Had they been able to expand their mental models to include transportation—being in the business of getting things and ideas from one place to another—they might (arguably) have been able to diversify into a variety of avenues. They could have become hugely successful if they had been able to meet such transportation needs as moving nonphysical things through phone, fax, and electrical lines; satellite and broadband technologies to move data; and communication tactics to help individuals move ideas from their heads into others.

The railroad analogy has an imperfect translation to the classic training industry, but it does serve to point out a need to see the future and latch onto it, or someone else will. Classic trainers and HRD professionals, who see themselves in the "training" business rather than in the business of helping people and organizations become successful, could see their functions diminished. Fortunately, an increasing number of trainers and learning and development professionals understand the challenge and are beginning to translate their "train" mentality into a "performance" mindset.

The demand for people who can help business leaders solve business issues quickly and efficiently will surely grow. These "performance consultants" will become an increasingly important venue to help leaders and executives increase organizational accomplishments. While many specialized roles associated with training and development (such as instructional designers and facilitators) can, and most likely will, be outsourced more, it does not appear that relationships with clients can (or should) be successfully outsourced. Internal performance consultants and human performance technology professionals are in the best positions to work with clients and continually identify and address performance needs. It is a very challenging job, to be sure, but it carries great rewards.

What Keeps Trainers from Adapting?

A number of general barriers keep some trainers from adapting to a performance approach. These barriers can be categorized based on the environmental and individual factors that need to be in place for performance (Gilbert, 1996). Environmental and individual factors, respectively, include:

Information and Feedback

- Clear direction and support from business and functional leaders are missing.
- Clear direction and expectation about what trainers are "supposed to be accomplishing"are absent.
- There is a lack of feedback regarding progress toward a performance focus.

Tools, Processes, Resources

- The right tools, processes, and resources are not present.

Incentives, Rewards, and Consequences

- The right incentives, rewards, and consequences are absent.

Skills, Knowledge, and Attitude

- They don't really know what "performance consulting" is.
- They don't know how to do it.
- They don't understand how organizations work systemically.
- They fear delving into areas beyond their current expertise.
- They lack knowledge of interventions outside of training.
- They don't have some of the key competencies necessary to be successful performance consultants.
- They are uncomfortable working with ambiguity.
- They are uncomfortable with the idea of having to work with executives, instead focusing almost exclusively on functional and departmental leadership.

Capacity

- They may not have the real capacity to act as performance consultants—this may be especially true of highly specialized trainers.

Motives

- They simply may not want to act as broader consultants, preferring to focus on detailed, focused issues.

Sometimes, the biggest barrier—the one most difficult to overcome—comes from the organization itself. Some companies simply won't let it happen. Even the best training cannot possibly be an effective strategic tool if key executives do not see it as such. In other words, the use of learning as a strategic business tool requires a supportive culture.

According to Judy Rosenblum, a former vice president and chief learning officer at the Coca-Cola Company, the strategic use of learning depends on the culture of the company and on what its leaders will stand for (Webber, 2000). Learning, she says, must be connected directly to the business; it must be embedded in processes, projects, and experiences. It is a strategic choice that doesn't just happen. It is a capability that requires skills to execute. It requires process. It requires leaders who value it.

If learning, with training and development as a subset, is to be a meaningful part of corporate or organizational future, it must "be of" the corporation and not just a functional accessory. The system that supports learning must be integrally connected with strategic support processes, such as human resources, which support primary corporate processes, such as sales, serving customers, and manufacturing products (Rummler & Brache, 1995).

A REVIEW OF HUMAN PERFORMANCE IMPROVEMENT (HPI)

The concept of viewing organizations as systems, of specifically identifying gaps between desired and actual performance and implementing focused solutions, goes by a number of names. In this chapter, it will be referred to using the following common names interchangeably: human performance improvement (HPI), human performance technology (HPT), and performance consulting. The first two terms refer to the body of knowledge and methods of performing processes to improve performance within organizations and to positively affect an organization's operational and financial results. Performance consulting generally refers to the process of carrying out HPI.

Thinking Holistically: Performance and Behavior

Before potential performance consultants worry about any specific model or process, they need to understand what it means to have a holistic performance mindset. In any organization, successful performance improvement interventions change the behaviors of people so that their performance accomplishes more of what the organization needs. Behavior, in this holistic sense, refers to much more than just overt action. What people actually do (that is, their observable behaviors) is inexorably linked with the environmental and individual factors that help or hinder their ability to act and accomplish meaningful results (Gilbert, 1996; Rummler & Brache, 1995).

A simple example serves to illustrate what a performance mindset might look like in practice. Mary is a homeowner who is working on a weekend shelving project for her garage. She fails to saw through a two-by-four piece of lumber with her handsaw, even though she worked at it for a while. She knows how to saw, she can perform the motions quite well, and she wants to cut the lumber. She knows the result she wants, but she still fails. She sits and asks: "Why is this lumber not cut?" She runs through her mental checklist:

- Is my goal clear? (Yes, I need to cut the lumber.)
- Do I know what I'm supposed to do? (Yes.)
- Can I see the progress, or lack of progress, being made? Do I get feedback? (Yes, I can see the wood is not cut.)
- Is the garage clean and set up appropriately for the task? (Yes.)
- Do I have the right tools? (Yes, I have a handsaw.)
- Is the tool working right? (No, I don't think so.)
- Have I followed all the right steps so far? (Yes, I'm pretty sure.)
- Is the job set up correctly? (Yes.)
- Do I have the right incentives? (Yes, cut lumber will help me build the shelves!)

Then Mary thinks about her personal situation. She further reflects by asking the following questions:

- Do I know how to saw? (Yes, I've been doing it for years!)
- Am I capable of sawing? (Yes.)
- Am I truly motivated to cut this thing? (Yes, I really want new shelves!)

After asking the questions, Mary decides to look more closely at the saw itself. Her tool-related question was the only one that yielded a negative answer. She discovers that the saw is excessively dull. She realizes that the dull teeth are the direct cause of her inability to saw through the lumber. She then thinks about what can be done to help her get the lumber cut as quickly and cheaply as possible. She looks at the alternatives. She could (a) get the saw sharpened, (b) get a new handsaw, (c) buy a new electric radial saw, or (d) hire a professional to do the sawing. She then examines the alternatives from a cost/benefit perspective:

- Saw sharpening can be done for fifteen dollars but takes about an hour to do.
- A comparable new handsaw costs about forty dollars, but it would be available as soon as she buys it.
- A new electric radial saw would cost over one hundred dollars.
- Hiring somebody would cost two hundred dollars, but they couldn't start until next Wednesday.

Mary weighs the alternatives and decides that she could drop the saw off to be sharpened, and then use the hour wait time to meet a friend for lunch at the new Mexican restaurant. The cost of her solution would be fifteen dollars plus one hour's time, but she feels that having the time to eat lunch with a friend offers sufficient benefit to balance the time factor costs. Her cost/benefit "analysis" points to sharpening the saw as her solution. With a newly sharpened saw, she makes quick work of the two-by-four. She's now a happy camper!

The point of this simple performance improvement example is that Mary had the competence to examine this problem using a performance approach. She accurately analyzed the situation, uncovered the true cause of the problem, and implemented an effective solution. She did not automatically assume that the problem required a specific type of solution. She knew that she had to look at the entire situation to get at the root cause. Mary has adeptly illustrated the approach of a performance consultant.

HPI focuses mostly on performance and accomplishments, with a secondary emphasis on behavior. It can be an elusive concept. It deals with outcomes, results, and accomplishments achieved by a person, group, or organization. Too often, the term *performance* is confused with behavior. A simple way to distinguish the difference between performance and behavior is to view performance as the end result and behavior as the means to that end. Behaviors are the actions that can contribute to accomplishments. Stated another way, behaviors are what people take with them, and accomplishments are what they leave behind (Rothwell, Hohne, & King, 2000).

A Performance Mindset

The process of performance consulting derives its value from its wholeness, the synergistic application of its diverse elements. Effective performance consultants are skilled at focusing on holistic solutions and solving business issues; they are, as Dana Robinson says, free of bias with regard to particular solutions and solution types (Robinson & Robinson, 1995). Consultants who come from within specific disciplines, such as HRD, must first overcome a perceived bias toward specific solutions. They need to be able to ask the right questions of the right people to get the systemic, multifaceted view of what is really causing the gap between desired and actual business and performance results. Once they can do this with competence, they can help clients design and implement appropriate solution mixes that hit upon all the necessary issues.

A Closer Look at HPI

Dana and Jim Robinson define performance consulting as a process in which a client and consultant partner to enhance workplace performance in support of business goals (Robinson & Robinson, 1998). Harold Stolovich and Erika Keeps (Stolovich & Keeps, 1999) present a much more comprehensive description that identifies most of the key elements involved. They define HPI (they call it HPT) as an engineering approach to attaining desired accomplishments from workers. Practitioners are those who adopt a systems view of performance gaps, systematically analyze both gap and system, and design cost-effective and efficient interventions that are based on analysis data, scientific knowledge, and documented precedents, in order to close the gap in the most desirable manner. Regardless of any specific definition, true human performance improvement approaches tend to share common characteristics:

- Viewed as *systemic* to account for the interconnectedness of organizational systems.

- Grounded in scientifically derived *theories* and the best empirical *evidence*.

- Focus on identifying and addressing *root causes* of human performance problems, based on the systemic *interaction* of performance factors.

- Distinguish between *performance* and *behavior*.

- Focus on *achievements* that workers and the system (i.e., organization) value.

- Define worthy performance as the *ratio* of the *value* of an accomplishment and the *costs* needed to achieve it (Gilbert, 1996).

- Rely on a *comprehensive analytical process* as the basis for solution identification, development, and implementation.

- Use appropriate *quantitative and qualitative data*, information, and measures to drive solution decisions.

- *Not bound* to the same solution(s) for all problems.

- Focus on engineering the *environment* to allow increased levels of human performance. Performance can be improved and remain improved if there is support from the environmental system of the organization (Gilbert, 1996; Rummler & Brache, 1995).

- Emphasize the role of observing and recording the actions of *exemplary performers* (i.e., those who regularly obtain corporately-valued results) and comparing those with the actions of more typical performers (Gilbert, 1996).

- Involve *expertise* that resides in diverse *teams*, not just within individuals, especially in solution implementation.

- Continually focus on assuring that organizational *leaders* learn the value of using the performance approach to help *solve business needs* (Dean, 1999).

A Rich and Diverse Pedigree

HPI is an umbrella discipline that draws its power from diversity and a rich history that dates to before the 1950s. It exists in a world in which the systems theories of Peter Senge and Marvin Weisbord live side by side with the ideas of Tom Gilbert, Geary Rummler and Robert Mager, who, in turn, live harmoniously on the same street that contains the older but still usable houses of B.F. Skinner, J. Edwards Deming, Peter Drucker, Malcolm

Knowles, and Don Kirkpatrick. These houses exist within a stone's throw of Dana and Jim Robinson's new complex, next to Allison Rossett's institute, about a half-mile south of Kurt Lewin's and Chris Argyris's modest abodes, and over the hill from Fredrick Taylor's ancient and boarded up mansion.

Ethan S. Sanders and Julie L. Ruggles (Sanders & Ruggles, 2000), Dana and James Robinson (1998) and Peter Dean and David Ripley (1997) have independently outlined the rich background disciplines and people who have contributed to the current state of the art. Table 6.1 provides a listing of the disciplines on which HPI is based, along with a brief description of each.

Key Tenets for Performance Consulting Practice

The concept of solving problems by identifying gaps between actual and desired conditions and figuring out how to bridge the gap is pretty simple. A person just needs to:

- know what HPI is all about,
- have a model and method of choice well in hand,
- be able to do performance consulting well,
- understand clients' business and needs, and
- do it.

It is simple in concept, yes, but not so easy in practice. It helps to realize some key tenets before diving into the detail of "how" the process is performed. There are a few key ideas that need to be considered in any performance consulting engagement, regardless of the exact methodology employed. These include alignment, leverage, human competence, exemplary performance, and simplicity. Each is discussed in turn.

Alignment counts. The tie to corporate strategic issues is critical. Any methodology used by a consultant must have the capability of assuring appropriate alignments and linkages throughout the organization. See chapter 2 for an extended discussion on this topic.

Leverage counts. Seek the best solutions that present the best "bang for the buck." Excellent consultants are constantly seeking to increase leverage by linking solutions.

Competence counts. Competence means that a performer accomplishes "worthy" performance within a socially defined context. This concept is, arguably, one of the most important concepts that anyone who wishes to be an exemplary performance consultant must be passionate about (Gilbert, 1996).

Tom Gilbert (1996, p. 29) defines competence in a social context, which provides a comparative judgment about the worth of performance. In a

Table 6.1
Contributing Fields to HPT

Discipline	Contribution to HPT
Behaviorism	HPT pioneers rooted their models in behaviorist concepts.
Diagnostic systems	Intervention choices are data-driven based on analysis process. Diagnosis before intervention.
Organizational learning, Instruct systems design	Instructional systems design theories formed a basis on which to build HPT models. Organizational learning models helped define complexities of transferring learning to job.
Systems theory	Highlights need to view performance in holistic view and the interdependent nature of systems.
Evaluation	HPT models consider the cost of interventions against the value obtained by the organization (benefit divided by cost). The theory allows performance consultants to demonstrate true value.
Management sciences	Evolving management science addresses social, motivational, and professional growth of employees balanced against firm needs.
Other theories	Communications theory, educational psychology, human development, human resource development, human resource management, instructional psychology, information technology, instructional systems design and technology, industrial psychology, learning theory, management theory, occupational education and development, systems theory, organizational learning, sociological theory, organizational design and development.

Adapted from: P. Dean & D. Ripley (Eds.) *Performance improvement pathfinders* (1997), (Washington, DC: ISPI).

business or organizational setting, the social context can be defined as "worthy performance"—performance that accomplishes a result valued by the organization but also does not cost too much, where cost includes financial issues, value issues, moral issues, and other relevant factors.

Relevant to this discussion is an acknowledgment that competencies and competence is not the same thing. The real difference between having *competency* and *being competent* lies in the final result—the accomplishment. A competency is the ability to perform. Competence is the ability to accomplish results in the real world by employing specific competencies. Competence is the successful execution of a competency for a meaningful result (Gilbert, 1996).

Say, for example, that the "world's greatest" team of bridge builders works smoothly to create the most beautiful and nearly indestructible bridge at the lowest possible cost. Is this team competent—maybe, maybe not. They are certainly efficient and possess a high level of bridge building competency. But, what if we told you that this "world's greatest" bridge building team built the bridge across the wrong river? The result did not meet the need—they are not competent in this case (Gilbert, 1996). Obviously, efficient behavior applied in the wrong direction can be even more incompetent than bumbling efforts in the right direction.

Competence, then, is defined by the context in which the results are needed. With the same basic competency, it is possible that a person can be competent in one setting but incompetent in another. That's why the setting and all of the factors that help or hinder accomplishment are so absolutely critical to consider. A focus on competence vs. competency really does not diminish the value of competency-based development, if for no other reason than a person can't possibly be competent without first having a level of competency. This logical path alone practically guarantees the role of learning, training, and development in the larger context—but always within the larger context, never standalone. The real goal of any HPI effort is to increase people's competence, not just their competency. This has tremendous implications for training and development because competence cannot possibly be viewed out of the context of the environment and the needs of the organization.

Exemplary Performers and Performance Models

Tom Gilbert (1996) and Jim and Dana Robinson (1995) discuss the importance of observing and recording the behaviors that *exemplary performers*—those within an organization who consistently accomplish results that the organization values—perform to get the results they do. The theory is simple.

Exemplary performers are the most competent performers. The differences between what exemplary performers do and what more typical performers do are rarely much different, yet the results they get can show great differences. Identifying and recording the things that exemplary performers do that are different from what more typical performers do presents enough information to develop contextually relevant "performance models." The process then is to uncover what is keeping typical performers from performing like exemplars, removing the barriers, and increasing the performance of the typical performers. Components of a performance model usually include the expected *result*, the *actions* performed by exemplars, the *competencies* on which those actions are based, and the *measures* used for evaluation. Table 6.2 represents a facsimile of a performance model as based upon a specific performance intervention (Wykes,

Table 6.2
Sample Performance Model

Dealer Assessor: Performance Model

Result Area . . . What Must Be Accomplished?	Competencies Required	Best Practices . . . How It Can Be Accomplished	Result Area Measures . . . Criteria for Excellence

Complete initial dealer assessment	• Analysis
	• Decision making
	• Information monitoring
	• Relationship building
		Definition: Select dealers for inclusion into the dealer group using solid, clear criteria
		1. Determine customer's potential service needs and select a dealer that meets those customer's needs
		  • Clarify the impact of choosing one dealer vs. another who is at or below an acceptable level of competence
		2. Apply key tenets to select appropriate dealers (based on capabilities, pricing, desire, support of FMC, minority business, and so on) and follow the process for selecting service providers.
		  • Use the following checkponts to select dealers:
		    1. Identify dealers who are capable and price competitive
		    2. Ascertain who desires to participate
		    3. Factor for historical business relationship
		    4. Identify geographic alignment and client presence
		    5. Identify dealers who regularly meet or exceed customer expectations
			• One page summary of assessment, with key points identified
			• Approval obtained before customer contract is finalized
			• Dealer capability measurement system in place

Adapted from: M. Wykes, J. March-Swets, & L. Rynbrandt. Performance analysis: Field operations management (2000), in J. Phillips (Ed.), *In action: Performance consulting and analysis* (pp. 135–153). Alexandria, VA: ASTD.

March-Swets, & Rynbrandt, 2000). Performance models differ from pure competency models in that they are based first on actions and behaviors performed by exemplary performers. The actions represent competent performance within a specific job setting; competencies are then derived from the actions.

The Value of Simplicity

Albert Einstein is often attributed with saying that everything should be as simple as possible—but not simpler. Bill Jensen (Jensen, 2000, p. 2) defines simplicity as the art of making complex things clear. Being simple doesn't mean being simplistic. It means focusing on the end result, knowing which things are really important, and using that as an ongoing guide. Knowing what is important to clients helps define the level of detail to be used to classify problems and recommend solutions.

At my current company, we often state that our job is to put a clear face on sometimes vague situations. We recently completed a large and complex corporate process improvement intervention, during which we had identified well over 1,500 comments related to barriers and disconnects that resulted in over sixty separate "problems" to be solved. We produced a very comprehensive solutions document that could be used as a guide for a full-blown implementation team. For our executive presentation, we boiled the issues into five different "buckets" of problems and presented three key actions to be done first by the executives before anything else. Our executive presentation was only thirty minutes long, and the executive summary was only four pages long (including two full-page graphics). During the meeting we suggested that the executives should do the following:

1. Choose and agree upon an executive owner for the process.
2. Select a full-time project director to make sure that the solutions are carried out (must be a director-level person with no other accountabilities).
3. Assure that the project director had the authority to select team members based on competence needed, not just "availability."

The executives came through, the project director came through, we supplied consultative help throughout the implementation phase, and the company benefited greatly as a result.

The Performance Consulting Process

The works of three leading HPI experts can help provide a solid base from which to actually "perform" performance consulting. First, the work of Dana and Jim Robinson (1995) provides a definition of the job and a working process for performance consulting. Second, the work of Thomas Gilbert helps assure that performance factors are addressed (Gilbert, 1996). Third, Geary Rummler and Allan Brache present a method and a mindset to help assure aligning and addressing of issues at all levels within a corporation (Rummler & Brache, 1995). Several points can be learned from each of these experts that add to the overall fabric of a workable performance consulting model.

Robinsons' model: The job and the process. Dana and Jim Robinson have defined and popularized the "job" and a practical process for performance consulting work. Their book, *Performance Consulting* (1995), should be the first book that anybody interested in performing effective HPI should read. Key points include the following:

- Build and maintain ongoing relationships with internal clients—independent of particular projects.
- Use very specific processes and tools to identify "should, is, and cause" information correctly and completely. *Should* information represents desired results. *Is* information defines the current state—what the actual current results are. Comparing the "should" to the "is" defines the performance gap. *Cause* information helps answer the question "What keeps performers from achieving desired results?"
- Enter engagements where the client's mind is. If they ask a "training" type question, then start there and attempt to uncover the underlying performance issues.
- Plan questions very carefully; they are some of the most powerful tools in a consultant's arsenal. And learn the skill of questioning well.
- Realize the client is the ultimate owner of a solution, not the performance consultant. Performance problems and solutions are analogous to a bus being driven by the client. The client both owns and drives that bus; the performance consultant is the navigator.

Gilbert: Factors for improving performance. Some key points (among many) to be learned from Gilbert include:

- Use exemplary performers to define what on-the-job actions should be performed.
- Focus on accomplishments, not just on actions.
- View performance in the light of the combined environmental and individual forces that shape them, particularly through the use of what Gilbert called the "Behavior Engineering Model" (Gilbert, 1996).

Rummler & Brache: Organizational levels/needs. Several things can be learned from Geary Rummler and Allan Brache, including the following points.

- Organizations are adaptive systems that are affected by numerous forces, both from outside and inside the organization.

- A number of performance variables, including individual performance factors, must be dealt with in order to effect any lasting performance improvements. Rummler and Brache (1995) define the organization, process, and job/performer levels as well as goals, design, and management (measurement) needs that must be addressed at each level.

The Process of Performance Consulting: Doing the Work

Figure 6.1 illustrates a combined process flow that integrates the best parts of models listed by several well-regarded sources (for example, Robinson & Robinson, 1995; Rothwell, 1996). Each phase of the process flow is discussed in turn.

Partnership with clients. This phase stresses the formation and growth of strong partnerships with clients (that is, those individuals in an organization who are accountable for achieving business goals). Usually this means partnering at the highest possible level in the organization. Strong relationships are important to continued trust and credibility. These partnerships are generally ongoing and can be independent of any particular performance consulting project. The relationship often opens the door to being able to perform the consulting process and can keep doors open if the improvement project should run into snags (Robinson & Robinson, 1995; Robinson & Robinson, 1998).

Entry phase. The Robinsons' model highlights formal entry into a consulting engagement for several important reasons. Entry can be either *reactive*—when someone contacts the consultant for help (often with a perceived "training" need), or *proactive*—when opportunities arise out of conversations with ongoing clients. Proactive entry is preferred because it focuses on business needs first (Robinson & Robinson, 1995).

Assessment and analysis. During this phase, the consultant analyzes present performance compared with desired performance to identify the gap.

Figure 6.1
Performance Consulting Process: A Simplified View

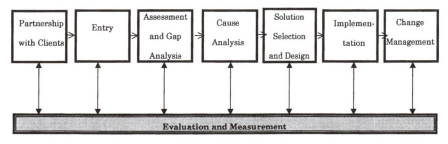

Based on: D.G. Robinson & J. Robinson, *Performance consulting: Moving beyond training* (1995), San Francisco: Berrett-Koehler.

Often this gap is presented in financial terms, business terms, and in terms of the performances needed to reach business goals. "Operational-should" goals are compared with "operational-is" accomplishments to define the gap. Performances are examined in terms of what is needed to obtain desired performance and compared with what people are actually doing that results in less than desired results. It is critical here to show the relationship between performances and obtaining objective goals. Also critical is to show linkages (or nonlinkages) of goals, objectives, and strategies. A key output of this stage includes clear identification of gaps.

A good tool to use during this stage is called a "relationship map" (Robinson & Robinson, 1995) as displayed in figure 6.2. This tool provides a visual reference to help ensure that a consultant examines operational issues

Figure 6.2
Simplified Relationship Map

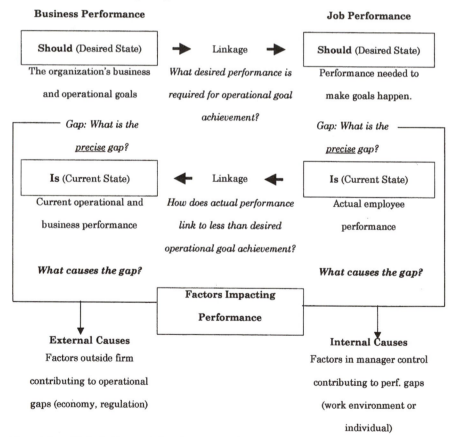

Adapted from: D.G. Robinson & J. Robinson. *Performance consulting: Moving beyond training* (1995), San Francisco: Berrett-Koehler.

(what should be vs. what really is); performances that affect the operational issues (what should be vs. what really is); and the causes, both internal and external, that affect performance. It is a useful tool to make sure that relevant relational factors are addressed.

Cause Analysis. During this phase the performance consultant defines why gaps exist and looks for the root cause factors that prevent good performance. A key output of this phase is a clear identification and presentation of key causes for gaps and their relationships. These causes can most effectively be categorized into six categories (Gilbert, 1996). Tom Gilbert illustrates this relationship in the form of what he termed the Behavioral Engineering Model (Gilbert, 1996, chap. 3), which suggests performance is a result of the interaction of a number of factors including:

- *Environmental factors* such as information flow (information and feedback); supporting systems, processes, and tools; rewards, incentives, and consequences.
- *Individual factors* such as skills, knowledge, attitudes, capabilities, and motivation of employees.

Figure 6.3 displays the relationship among these factors. The top row represents *environmental* factors (provided by the organization) and *individual* factors (provided by individual performers), which must be addressed

Figure 6.3
Factors for Performance

Environment Factors: (What the organization provides)	1. Information: Expectations and Feedback (Clear expectations and appropriate feedback)	2. Tools, Systems Processes, Resources, Space, and Technology	3. Incentives: Rewards and Consequences (Financial and Nonfinancial)
Individual Factors: (What the individual provides)	4. Skills, Knowledge, and Attitudes	5. Individual Capacity	6. Motivation (Intrinsic—within the person—and extrinsic)

Based on: T. Gilbert (1996). *Human competence: Engineering worthy performance* (Tribute Edition) Washington, DC: ISPI. Used with permission, the International Society for Performance Improvement, © 1996.

and work together to provide an environment allowing high levels of performance. If any factors are not tackled appropriately, performance is
likely to suffer.

The point here is that these factors are interdependent. Environmental
factors must match with individual factors. For example, direction given
by management must match the skills of the people who are to carry out the
tasks. And incentives offered must match the motives and needs of people,
etc. (Dean, 1999; Gilbert, 1996).

During analysis, I have found that Gilbert's Behavior Engineering
Model works best when combined with Geary Rummler and Alan Brache's
concepts and definitions concerning levels within organizations and the
needs that must be filled for performance to happen. Rummler & Brache
view each organization as a system that must continually adapt to numerous forces from outside and from within in order to survive and grow. It can
only do this if a number of performance variables are aligned and addressed (Rummler & Brache, 1995; Rummler, 1998). Rummler (1998) usually defines these components in the form of a matrix that has two
dimensions: (a) the three *levels* of performance, and (b) the performance
needs that must be satisfied within those levels.

Three levels must be aligned—the organization, process, and job/per-
former level. Within each level, three types of needs must be aligned:

- Goals—All three levels need clear goals and standards that reflect customers' expectations.
- Design—All three levels must have structures that enable goals to be met.
- Management (and measurement)—Each level needs a management system and
  practices to ensure focus and progress toward goals.

Furthermore, combining the three levels with the three types of needs
yields a matrix that is made up of nine performance variables (Rummler &
Brache, 1995). The needs and levels interrelate as follows:

Organization Level

- Goals—Are organizational goals and objectives clear?
- Design—Is the organization structured for efficiency and effectiveness?
- Management—Are efficient systems in place to monitor and manage perfor-
  mance?

Process Level

The process level refers to the cross-functional processes by which work
gets done. Examples include the product development process, order fulfillment process, and sales process. These *must* be aligned with the organization level.

- Goals—Do the necessary processes exist? Are goals aligned with organization goals?

- Design—Are processes well designed to meet requirements?

- Management—Do the right measures and systems exist to monitor and manage performance?

Job/Performer Level

The job/performer level *must* likewise be aligned with the process level.

- Goals—Do the right jobs exist to perform processes? Are job goals aligned with process goals?

- Design—Are the jobs designed to allow effective and efficient performance?

- Management—Are environmental and individual factors aligned to allow top performance to take place? Are the right measures in place? Is performance monitored and are deviations diagnosed and corrected?

The point, as Rummler (1998) suggests, is that alignment among all of the levels and needs is critical for performance improvement to take place. The matrix, as a performance consulting tool, helps to ensure that the necessary performance variables are satisfied. The performance matrix also provides a convenient framework from which to design and ask systemic organizational diagnosis questions. Figure 6.4 shows an example of how this "level and needs thinking" can be applied to help identify and categorize key barriers to performance in a systemic way. The example is an abridged version of a categorization tool used by my current company's performance consultants during a large consulting engagement.

Solution selection and design. During the solution selection and design phase, the consultant works with client representatives and subject matter experts to select an appropriate mix of solutions designed to effectively lessen performance gaps. Typically, solutions may include varied interventions based on barriers to success uncovered during the causal analysis. Solutions often include a mix of policy changes, clarifications, staffing, training, technology solutions, changes to reward, measurement and reward/consequence systems. The output of this phase often includes a simple, clear executive summary, solution documentation including prioritized solutions that are matched with the problems they are solving, cost/benefit analysis, resource needs, and other details as needed. The quality and comprehensiveness of the solution mix is directly related to the quality of the outputs generated during the analysis phase.

Implementation. During implementation the consultant works with the client to help assure that solutions are carried out efficiently and effectively. It is critical in this phase that the client actually owns the benefit derived from the solutions. Chances of success are related to clients' perceptions and involvement. If clients feel that solutions are being done *to* them, the

Figure 6.4
Barriers to Performance Example

	Focus Issues	Design Issues	Management and Measurement Issues
Organization level barriers	• Lack of clarity about org. strategy • Many different initiatives at once; executive support perceived as spotty • Action mainly in crisis	• Many alignments by function, not process • Too many points of contact for customers	• Incentives are functionally focused, not process focused • No incentive to forego short-term gain for future gain
Process level barriers	• Process goals have internal focus vs. final focus on satisfaction • Sales makes commitments without checking ability to deliver	• Scheduling often driven by rush needs • Complexities: 150 actions per order	• Lack of action taken • Lack of skill/process match • Conflicting incentives/rewards • Tools not linked
Job performer level barriers	• Job goals not linked to integrated process standards—tend to be linked to narrower goals • Individual measures inconsistently linked	• Department reps. lack decision authority • Work overload • Some accountable for things beyond control	• Info. / feedback • Tools / process / resource • Incentive • Skill / knowledge • Capacity / motives

Adapted from: Unpublished, L. Michael Wykes, Barriers to performance (2000), which is based primarily upon G.A. & Rummler A. Brache, *Improving performance* (1995, 2nd ed.). San Francisco: Jossey-Bass, p. 27.

chances for successful follow-through are far less likely than if they perceive that solutions are being done *with* them or *by* them.

Key outputs of this phase include attainment of project plan steps and measures and the ultimate increases in performance as outlined during the entry and analysis phases. The implementation phase can range from very short periods (a week or two) to two months (for a focused in-plant manufacturing project) to over a year (for a large corporate process improvement project). Most of the work—especially the detail work on an overall performance improvement project—occurs during the implementation phase. If done correctly, diverse and specialized teams comprised of client representatives and intervention specialists do this work. The performance consultant often acts as a process consultant and confidant to the chosen project leader.

This phase can cause concern among trainers. Much of the actual expertise for implementing a particular solution or mix of solutions lies outside of the skill set that many HRD professionals have. During this phase, the performance consultant often acts as an intervention broker and as a project manager who helps make sure that individual interventions combine to solve issues systemically. Interventions can be classified by:

- The *kind* of performance change the intervention merits. Interventions can be implemented to establish performance (create new performance), improve existing performance, maintain performance, or extinguish performance (eliminate undesired performance). (Langdon, Whiteside, & McKenna, 1999).

- The intended *audience level*. An individual, work groups, processes, or business units may comprise the audience (Langdon, Whiteside, & McKenna, 1999).

In a well-done performance consulting process, there should be a direct correlation between the major barriers uncovered during a performance analysis and the specific mix of interventions chosen to eliminate those barriers to allow for improved performance.

According to Robinson (Robinson, 2000), about 22 percent of performance-focused interventions are performed primarily by performance consultants (mostly when the focus is on eliminating skill or knowledge gaps), and about 48 percent are done as a joint responsibility of the client group and the consultant. Common focus areas for interventions follow:

- training and development,
- job aids,
- HR interventions—performance management, selection systems, and incentive plans,
- work-flow process redesign and job redesign, and
- major business initiatives related to manufacturing, order fulfillment, and other issues.

Change management. The "step" of managing the change process is not called out separately in many models—it is often incorporated into the general implementation phase. Rothwell (1996) and others, however, find it significantly important to call out. Managing the process with the client is often the most difficult step to complete successfully. During this step, the consultant monitors progress and helps ensure that individuals and groups get the information they need. Consultants also guarantee that key stakeholders are continually involved in the process. The best consultants are able to repeatedly maintain relationships with clients (at the highest levels), build helpful support, and gain buy-in from executives and other corporate leadership.

Evaluation and measurement. This step is really both an end and a beginning. It puts a cap on the current engagement and sets the stage for possible further engagements. During this step, the consultant compares actual goal and objective attainment with specific accomplishments that were defined in the entry and assessment phases. This phase asks the questions: Did you get the results you wanted? If not, why? What needs to be done now? The consultant uses a variety of qualitative and quantitative data collection and analysis techniques to perform measurement and evaluation.

A key point to remember is that measurement alone is *not* evaluation. An evaluation occurs only when a measurement is compared to a standard or to a desired goal. This gives a reading of the relative worth of an intervention. Let's say, for example, that you ordered a replacement wheel for a child's metal wagon. When the wagon wheel was delivered, you discover that it measures eight feet in diameter. That measure alone means nothing until you compare it to a standard of eight inches. The evaluative statement would indicate that this is a really big wheel! The measure was eight feet—the evaluation indicates that this would be unacceptable for the intended use, no matter how unique an eight-foot diameter wheel might be. This wheel would be evaluated as acceptable for a well-known child's wagon maker that actually did make an oversized wagon, with eight-foot wheels, as a demonstration. Measures simply tell "what is." An evaluation defines the value and worth in a specific situation.

Evaluation is actually planned during the assessment phase but is carried out during the performance consulting process. Evaluation can be done during the process to guide and shape the ongoing actions (that is, formative evaluation). It is also performed after an intervention has been completed to gauge the intervention's impact on critical measures (that is, summative evaluation).

THE PERFORMANCE CONSULTING JOB

Before the 1980s the job title of "performance consultant" really did not exist. But changing business conditions fueled an increasing need for a role that partnered with executives and line management, had a strong focus on performance improvement, and had the ability to help leaders solve business problems quickly and efficiently. Today, numerous organizations incorporate people who formally or informally act as "performance consultants" or performance technologists, although not necessarily under those titles. Titles of people who do performance consulting type of functions can be as varied as learning services consultant, relationship manager, performance technologist, HR consultant, learning and performance advisor, and manager of performance strategies (Robinson & Robinson, 1999). While the majority of these jobs exist within HR departments they may also organizationally fit under other corporate functions such as corporate quality. They could even exist as independent profit centers.

Accountabilities

Perhaps the easiest way to discuss what a performance consultant actually does is to talk about it in terms of the job outputs that performance consultants are generally called upon to produce. According to an ongoing study conducted by Partners in Change, Inc. (Robinson & Robinson, 1999; Robinson, 2000), the role of performance consulting is most frequently held accountable for five major job outputs. As outlined in this section, within each accountability, a variety of behaviors, techniques, and success criteria is used (Robinson & Robinson, 1999).

1. Form and grow partnerships with sustained clients

Exemplary performance consultant behaviors:

- Participate in staff meetings and strategic planning meetings.
- Listen to the client's (either internal or external) concerns and respond quickly.
- Use meetings with clients on existing situations to discuss performance issues.
- Keep up with business and industry trends.

Techniques used:

- Ask questions to raise awareness about what could be done to help the client's situation.
- Use hard numbers about the cost of a problem to make a business case for what needs to happen.

Success criteria:

- Ratings from external customer satisfaction surveys.
- Included in high profile meetings with clients.
- Number of performance improvement projects being solicited.
- Repeat projects with same clients.

2. Identify and qualify opportunities for performance improvement

This accountability is typically included in the former. However, it was separated here for emphasis.

3. Conduct performance assessments, including gap and cause analysis

Data collection methods include:
- One-on-one interviews
- Focus groups
- Surveys
- Observation

Success Criteria:

- Acceptance of data by client
- Positive feedback from client
- Improved business results and/or on-the-job performance
- Meet deadlines

4. Manage multiple performance change interventions

Types of projects managed:
- Providing training and development solutions, including job aids
- Human resources change projects including: performance management, selection systems, incentive plans
- Workflow and process redesign
- Major business initiatives

Best practices:
- Use project management approach with a project charter.
- Involve performers and their managers as much as possible.
- Contract for outside resources.
- Serve as liaison to client and team members.
- Update client on regular basis.

Success Criteria:
- Job performance of target group(s) has improved.
- Positive feedback is received.
- Project moves ahead according to plan and objectives.
- Project timelines are met.

5. Measure the results of performance improvement interventions

It is important to note that research shows about only one-half of performance consulting departments are systematically measuring performance change and operational results (Robinson & Robinson, 1999). Nonetheless, best practices and success criteria include the following.

Best Practices:

- Design measures and methods into contract with the client.
- Design and use front-end and postintervention measures.
- Use accepted measurement techniques.
- Compare pre and postdata.
- Track projects against predetermined measures.
- Use the organization's current measures as much as possible for Level 4 results measurement (Kirkpatrick, 1994).

Success Criteria:

- Measurement activities move ahead according to the plan.
- Client is satisfied with measurement information.
- Intervention goals were achieved.
- Client supports additional measurement project.

Competence and Competencies

Exemplary performance consultants are competent in a number of areas. They regularly perform job actions to produce valued outputs by employing a number of key competencies. These competencies are arranged roughly around the aforementioned accountabilities.

1. Relationship Builder

Form and grow partnerships with sustained clients and identify and qualify opportunities for performance improvement.

- Industry, business, and organization knowledge (i.e., knowing the business, how corporate strategies and processes link, and organizational dynamics)
- Leadership and interpersonal skills
- Systems thinking
- Technological skill
- Problem solving skill
- Intervention skills (i.e., applying a variety of interventions to solve performance problems)
- Negotiating and contracting skills
- Advocacy and buy-in skills
- Ability to see the "big picture"
- Consulting skills (i.e., ability to uncover stakeholder needs and to provide insights on how to efficiently and effectively achieve results)
- Relationship building

2. Analyst

Conduct performance assessments. This includes performing a gap and cause analysis.

- Performance analysis (i.e., comparing desired to actual performance to identify performance gaps and opportunities)
- Needs analysis survey design
- Competency identification
- Questioning and interviewing skills
- Data manipulation skills, or the ability to handle data and produce effective reports
- Analytical synthesis, or the ability to quickly break down data and synthesize meaning
- Work environment analysis (i.e., using a systemic viewpoint to examine systems)
- Individual and environmental factor analysis (i.e., using systematic tools to examine and report on individual and environmental factors that affect performance)

3. Intervention Specialist

Manage multiple organizational or performance-change interventions simultaneously.

- Performance intervention interpretation, or finding useful meaning in performance findings and communicating them clearly to stakeholders/clients
- Intervention selection (i.e., picking a variety of performance improvement interventions to address root causes)
- Performance change interpretation, or forecasting and analyzing the effects of interventions
- Ability to assess relationships among interventions (i.e., examining the effects of multiple interventions on the organization and their interactions with customers, suppliers, and workers)
- Ability to identify critical business issues and changes
- Goal implementation, or converting goals into specific actions, despite conflicting priorities, lack of resources, or ambiguity
- Change impetus, or determine what needs to be changed
- Communication (i.e., the ability to communicate effectively in organizations through channels, both informal and formal)
- Group dynamics and process
- Process consultation
- Facilitation

4. Evaluator

Measure the results of performance improvement interventions in order to establish efficacy.

- Evaluation (i.e., the ability to design and implement defensible evaluation processes)
- Performance gap evaluation
- Ability to evaluate results against organizational goals
- Standard setting
- Assessing impact on culture
- Human performance improvement intervention reviewing skills
- Feedback skills

PUTTING IT INTO ACTION

Successful introduction and use of HPI to increase business performance requires a planned, thoughtful approach. Many trainers and HRD professionals have received a mandate from their leaders to go forth and "do" performance consulting. In response, they read some books and articles, do the best they can to develop their process, design professional-looking presentation materials, and begin to pitch the product throughout the organization. The lucky ones learn very quickly what any successful sales person knows—trying to sell a product that has no specific branding to clients who may not even know what it is, who may not even know they need it, let alone what it can do for them, is a path doomed to fail.

Any approach to marketing HPI within an organization should be built with a firm realization that clients want results—their results. They need their problems solved. They want to hear things in their language. They are interested in the meaningful results of a process—always—not in the process itself.

Define Your Process, Model, and Method

Successful practitioners decide which HPI model and approach they will use, and they use it as a basis from which to evolve. For example, when we first started a performance consulting practice at my current company in 1996, we centered on a model proposed by the Dana and Jim Robinson (Robinson & Robinson, 1995) as a basic methodology. We had several consultants who had HR experience but little actual performance consulting experience. The Robinson's model provided a clear process that our new performance consultants could use even if they didn't fully understand its genesis. As our departmental expertise, success ratio, and skills have grown, we have developed a broad, flexible model. It is still based roughly on the Robinsons' model but also includes elements from Tom Gilbert and Geary Rummler's concepts (especially for large process improvement efforts). It is a flexible process, which can be adapted to fit both large and small performance improvement jobs within our specific corporate environment.

Do a Performance Audit

An excellent "first step" for a training organization that wishes to transition into a performance focus is to perform a performance audit on itself. This approach, originally proposed by Tom Gilbert (1996), highlights accomplishments, exemplary performance, and a comparison with typical performance. The audit results in a pretty good picture of the competence of existing members as compared to ideal performance. Gilbert's performance audit steps include the following:

1. Identifying accomplishments (what the system is currently accomplishing)
2. Identifying requirements (what the system needs to have done)
3. Identifying exemplary performance (what the realistic potential is)
4. Measuring exemplary performance
5. Measuring typical performance
6. Computing the potential for improving performance (the discrepancy between exemplary and typical performance)
7. Translating this potential into a measure of economic potential (e.g., savings or improvement associated with exemplary performance)

This approach is unique because it focuses on the differences between exemplary (i.e., the best performers who consistently achieve results the organization needs) and typical performers. Doing this puts the improvement opportunity squarely on leveraging the performance of "okay" performers and increasing their performance, sometimes incrementally, to increase ultimate results. Of course, increasing their performance brings us right back to the environmental and individual issues that must be in place to allow that performance to happen!

Clarify Roles

This step is fairly straightforward. Clarify who is going to do the work, who's going to help them, and who is going to own it from the client's perspective.

Develop a Clear "Elevator Conversation"

It is really important to be painfully clear and succinct in the definition of "what you do." Jim Fuller (1998) defines a good definition as one that can be said to someone in a thirty-second elevator ride. In other words, keep it free of HR jargon! Here is an example (one I've used countless times) to explain what performance consultants do:

We use a comprehensive approach to identify barriers that prevent people from reaching business results the organization needs. We then help clients eliminate those barriers so people can perform better to reach or exceed those results. And we can do this pretty quickly. (Throwing in the word *quickly* usually brightens a potential client's eyes. If the word *quick* is used it must be backed by a real capacity.)

One other concise definition centers on what a successful performance improvement department does. This one is a bit wordier; it stretches the thirty-second limit a bit:

We use a highly adaptable process to help clients solve business problems. We do this quickly and accurately. Because we meld process-thinking with human performance technology, we can analyze and present a picture of issues and solutions to address all factors necessary to increase peoples' ability to meet or exceed business goals at all levels in the organization.

Yet another thirty-second version could be built around questions. Consider the following example:

We follow a process that helps you, the client, answer several questions:

- What business results do you need?
- What is the gap—if any—between the results you need and the results you are getting?
- What keeps workers from getting the results you need?
- How can we fix things so you can get the results you need?
- How will we know when it's fixed?

Whatever defining statement is chosen, it must be clear and capable of being portrayed without the use of visuals or graphics. Sometimes, it is really helpful to have even shorter catch phrases to garner your client's attention, such as:

- We help make the obvious, painfully obvious. (Szara, 2000)
- We put a visual face on vague problems.
- We use simple tools, but we use them very, very well.

Understand the Company's Business

It is absolutely critical to have a working knowledge of the organization's business and the various processes it uses to produce successful outputs. This does not mean becoming a business expert, but it does mean having the language that internal business clients speak. It is also important that a performance consultant is able to vary his/her speech to accommodate different audiences and audience levels.

Form Alliances with Key Leaders and Early Adopters

It is very important to form alliances and build relationships with key executives. It is also key to solidify a relationship with an influential corporate champion in a core business process like products sold, product or services manufactured and delivered, or customers satisfied (Rummler & Brache, 1995).

Position Your Role

Results count. They speak loudly. Selling HPI within an organization is a continual process that doesn't rely on the "big presentation" to prove value. Selling results by showing capability to get results presents a paradox when a department first wants to become a performance-focused organization. It is sometimes hard to initiate first projects. There are two approaches that can be taken, according to Jim Fuller (1998).

The first approach is what Fuller calls a head-on approach. He suggests that this approach is often best and can be described in the form of a competency called "reframing," (Robinson & Robinson, 1995) or turning clients' training requests into performance requests. When clients ask for a training solution, the consultant asks appropriate questions to try identifying a performance need behind the request. This presents a potential opportunity to explain the HPT approach and how it could get to the root of the client's problems. The consultant asks permission to try using an HPT approach. If that permission is not granted, the consultant simply delivers what the client wants and moves on to the next potential client. Eventually, someone who's willing to give it a shot will surface!

A second approach is called the end-run approach (Fuller, 1998). Here the consultant applies the HPT approach to a client's request . . . even though the client may have only asked for training. The consultant does not really ask for "permission" to perform HPI; he or she just does it. This isn't really deceptive because the consultant ends up giving the clients more than they asked for—to the client's benefit.

Watch Out for Barriers

Any time a training-to-performance paradigm shift is attempted, some barriers may arise. For example, line training managers, associated with particular business units may offer some resistance because they might perceive HPI as a threat to their job measures. They are often measured by standard training type criteria: numbers of people trained, numbers of courses, and so on, and may be reluctant to buy into a broader approach, especially if they have no support from above. A good approach to alleviate this problem is to discuss how HPT can benefit their enterprise and attempt to form a working partnership.

Traditional trainers may fear the loss of their jobs or a change in what they have become accustomed to. In this scenario, stress that training is still a very needed and valid solution when lack of knowledge is a clearly identified barrier. Good instructional systems design and training delivery will always be necessary. Trainers often lack of knowledge about noninstructional solutions. They may be unfamiliar with compensation systems, process design, ergonomics, incentive systems, and information systems. Performance consultants act more as brokers than "doers." They don't have to be experts, but they do have to know who the experts are and must have the ability to bring those functions in as needed as part of multidisciplinary solution implementation teams.

Turf battles can tear a worthwhile effort apart if clear ownership, roles, and benefits are not established up front. Clarifying at the highest levels within the organization where a performance consulting function should reside can lessen potential turf battles. It is also important, especially for the initiator of the change, to assure that win-win scenarios are developed with just about every group that may feel threatened.

FINAL THOUGHTS

The task of becoming a proficient performance consultant isn't necessarily an easy one, nor is it quick. The path "from here to there" is laden with potential pitfalls and false roads. Fortunately, though, becoming skilled at exhibiting a performance focus is a bit like learning to play a banjo. If you learn a few simple chords pretty well, you can begin to pick out a few recognizable tunes, and the more you practice the better you get. Being a really, really good banjo picker, however, takes quite a bit of practice before you feel good about performing in front of a live audience.

Reading the information presented in this chapter really only gives you a license to practice. Any reader will need to ensure that the performance variables needed to encourage a performance focus are in place, both externally (that is, in the work environment) and internally. The information itself is a dry, lifeless thing until through your competence you bring it to life.

BIBLIOGRAPHY

Dean, P. (Ed.). (1999). *Performance engineering at work*. Washington, DC: International Society of Performance Improvement.

Dean, P., & Ripley, D. (Eds.). (1997). *Performance improvement pathfinders*. Washington, DC: International Society of Performance Improvement.

Fuller, J. (1998). Making the transition to a focus on performance. In D.G. Robinson and J. Robinson (1998). *Moving from training to performance: A practical guidebook*. San Francisco: American Society of Training and Development and Berrett-Koehler.

Gilbert, T. (1996). *Human competence: Engineering worthy performance*. (Tribute Ed.). Washington, DC: International Society for Performance Improvement.

Jensen, W.D. (2000). *Simplicity*. New York: Perseus.

Kirkpatrick, D.L. (1994). *Evaluating training programs: The four levels*. San Francisco: Berrett-Koehler.

Langdon, D., Whiteside, K., & McKenna, M. (1999). *Intervention resource guide: 50 performance improvement tools*. San Francisco: Jossey-Bass/Pfeiffer.

Phillips, J. (1998). *Handbook of training evaluation and measurement methods*. (3rd ed.). Washington, DC: Gulf Publishing and American Society of Training and Development.

Phillips, J. (Ed.). (2000). *In action: Performance consulting and analysis*. Alexandria, VA: American Society of Training and Development.

Robinson, J. (2000). The evolving performance consultant job: A four-year study. Pittsburgh, PA: Partners in Change, Inc.

Robinson, D.G., & Robinson, J. (1995). *Performance consulting: Moving beyond training*. San Francisco: Berrett-Koehler.

Robinson, D.G., & Robinson, J. (1998). *Moving from training to performance: A practical guidebook*. San Francisco: American Society of Training and Development and Berrett-Koehler.

Robinson, J., & Robinson, D.G. (1999). Performance consultant: The job. In H.D. Stolovich, & E.J. Keeps, Eds.), *Handbook of human performance technology* (pp. 713–729). San Francisco: International Society of Performance Improvement and Jossey-Bass.

Rossett, A. (1999). *First things fast: A handbook for performance analysis*. San Francisco: Jossey-Bass Pfeiffer.

Rothwell, W. (Ed.). (1996). *ASTD models for human performance improvement*. Washington, DC: American Society of Training and Development.

Rothwell, W., Hohne, C., & King, S. (2000). *Human performance improvement: Building practitioner competence*. Houston: Gulf.

Rummler, G. (1998). The three levels of alignment. In D.G. Robinson & J. Robinson (Eds.), *Moving from training to performance: A practical guidebook* (pp. 13–35). San Francisco: American Society of Training and Development and Berrett-Koehler.

Rummler, G.A., and Brache, A. (1995). *Improving performance: How to manage the white space on the organization chart* (2nd ed.). San Francisco: Jossey-Bass.

Sanders, E.S., & Ruggles, J.L. (2000). HPI soup. *Training and Development Journal*, 45(6), 26–36.

Stolovich, H.D., & Keeps, E.J. (Eds.) (1999). *Handbook of human performance technology*. San Francisco: International Society of Performance Improvement and Jossey-Bass.

Szara, G. (2000, March). *How to do quick performance analysis that leads to real results: Case studies in adaptation at Steelcase, Inc.* Paper presented at the annual meeting of the International Society for Performance Improvement, Dallas, TX.

Training Industry Report 2000. (2000, October). *Training: Special industry report.* Minneapolis, MN: Lakewood.

van Adelsberg, D. & Trolly, E.A. (1999). *Running training like a business: Delivering unmistakable value,* San Francisco: Berrett-Koehler.

Webber, A. (2000). Will companies ever learn? *Fast Company, 39,* 274–282.

Wykes, M. (1998). Performance analysts at Steelcase. In D.G. Robinson & J. Robinson (Eds.), *Moving from training to performance: A practical guidebook* (pp. 78–93). San Francisco: American Society of Training and Development and Berrett-Koehler.

Wykes, M., March-Swets, J., & Rynbrandt, L. (2000). Performance analysis: Field operations management. In Phillips, J. (Ed.), *In action: Performance consulting and analysis* (pp. 135–153). Alexandria, VA: American Society of Training and Development.

Chapter 7

RAISING THE BAR: HIGH-IMPACT TRAINER ROLES IN THE NEW WORKPLACE

Jennifer W. Guidry

Trainers have worn many hats in the workplace. The most traditional, albeit important, roles have been that of strategist, analyst, designer, facilitator, and administrator (Noe, 1999). To achieve basic competence as a trainer, it is important to perform these traditional roles well, either within the training department or by bringing in outside resources to fill in the gaps.

However, competence in these conventional roles alone is not sufficient to perform effectively in today's workplace. Like all employees in the highly competitive business environment, trainers are faced with the requirement to do more than simply meet customer expectations. Indeed, the bar for trainers has been raised (Bachler, 1997). Trainers must not only meet customer expectations, but also exceed them, and then innovate to impact and maintain their customer base. Consequently, trainers must raise the bar on their own performance in order to achieve maximum impact in their organizations.

To exceed expectations and create new methods, trainers must be more sophisticated in their approach, even in their traditional roles. Furthermore, they must learn to master some important, but less clearly defined, new roles. The role of trainer has expanded to include that of "change ambassador," "marketer," and even "spiritual leader" for the organization, due to the past twenty years of corporate downsizing, rightsizing, and reengineering. In other words, more than ever before, trainers are being asked to speak to the human side of business and to effectively address the "people issues" that arise out of organizational turmoil.

As change ambassadors, trainers are being asked to champion major organizational initiatives and to provide employees with practical business tools and human strategies to cope with these changes. As marketers, trainers increasingly find it necessary to apply marketing techniques within the organization to effectively reach their audiences and thereby gain buy-in, participation, and customer loyalty. And as spiritual leaders, trainers must help employees find meaning and purpose in their work lives and encourage them to "keep the faith" despite the obstacles faced in today's sometimes spiritually bereft organizations. This role clearly needs to be handled carefully, responsibly, and effectively.

These three more contemporary trainer roles (change ambassador, marketer, and spiritual leader) are quickly becoming essential competencies. According to recent research assessing trainer competencies, trainers must not only be able (a) to think strategically and improve customer focus, but must also be able (b) to champion new goals, (c) to maintain employees' enthusiasm, and (d) to encourage changes in behavior, even in the light of disappointment and disillusionment (Galagan & Salopek, 2000).

This chapter will describe both the traditional roles and the "new" roles of trainers, based largely on personal experience, and will discuss how becoming more proficient in these roles not only can help trainers innovate to achieve high impact in the new workplace, but also to perform their work on a higher, more meaningful level. This effort is what it will take to be part of training's "new guard" at the leading edge of training, where trainers bring their whole selves to their work, push themselves creatively to improve, and work from the heart and soul (Galagan & Salopek, 2000).

CHANGING PERCEPTIONS IN TRAINING

Tulane University in New Orleans offers a course on learning and development as part of its human resources certificate program. The course is a comprehensive overview of training issues, skills, and techniques in the training and development field. When teaching this course, I notice that some of the students initially seem to think the course will be easy, and that they think of the trainer in the most traditional sense—a job skills trainer with a limited role in an organization.

It is amazing how many workplace stereotypes many of the students already hold in their minds—that training is too focused on ineffective "touchy-feely" stuff and that training isn't necessarily connected with organizational strategy. By the end of the course, however, most students look at training from a different perspective. They become more aware of the broadened role of trainers in organizations—from teaching skills and knowledge, to linking training to business needs, to using training to create and share knowledge (Martocchio & Baldwin, 1997). The students also have explored the role of the trainer beyond the most basic competencies and discussed the idea of trainer as change ambassador, marketer, and spiritual leader. This was illustrated by the response of a student to a question on the final exam asking about the most significant concept learned during the course. The student wrote:

> The most significant idea I learned this semester is the simple fact that the training profession is such a detailed, cognitive, and large industry. That is not to say that I thought that people trained themselves, but I just assumed that trainers were there to teach the mechanics of a job to a group of employees who aren't going to listen anyway. Instead I realized that trainers exist on all different knowledge, skill, and talent levels and the best ones are some of the most important people in business. A trainer is a spiritual leader who can do everything from increase capital (ROI, cost benefit) to help out the emotional stance of an employee (affective attitudes.)

As so astutely observed by the student, the trainer is someone who wears multiple hats and has a direct connection to the financial and spiritual wellbeing of the company and its employees. It is important that all trainers recognize this expanded scope of their responsibilities.

THE TRAINER AS STRATEGIST

The first, more traditional role of trainer is that of *strategist*. While this is a critical role for effective trainers, it is, unfortunately, often limited or ignored completely in today's businesses and training departments. Trainers frequently suffer from the same problem that other employees have—the inability to see their job from the more global perspective of how it fits into the overall organization's mission, vision, and values. Many trainers often get caught up in the day-to-day responsibilities of their jobs—the workshop at hand, the quarterly calendar of training sessions, the workbooks to bind together, and so on. Moreover, the senior managers they work with often neglect the broader view as well.

Such a myopic perspective can prevent training and development from taking a more respected place in the organization and causes the leadership to doubt the people and processes that support learning in the organization (Caudron, 2000). Training, when it is not linked to strategic goals, can be viewed as a hassle, a waste of time, something that the training department cooked up (Mager, 1996). Even when it has the appearance of top management support, line managers are often not asked how the training will help them reach their goals, so it is simply viewed as a mandated disruption that they will comply with, but not truly commit to or participate in.

Recently, one of my clients acknowledged that they have often taken a "shotgun," rather than a strategic approach to training. They have assessed a particular content need, and then asked for a program to fit that need.

Training was viewed as important because it builds the basic competence of the managers, but it was not directly related to the overall business strategy of the organization in terms of employee retention or skill development. Now, however, after some prodding, this senior management team is beginning to consider how training might impact their current business strategy and what steps can be taken to further their business goals through training, internal communication and marketing, and employee development.

It is important for training to be implemented as part of a strategic training plan, rather than "by calendar." To achieve maximum impact, training managers should use appropriate methods to ensure a more strategic approach. For example, they can create an actual one- to two-year training plan that lists objectives for the training department based on overall company objectives. The plan should, however, maintain enough flexibility that the department can deliver training on an as-needed basis as a consequence of changes in the business environment. The plan also can be used to establish training priorities over time and to reflect the goals and objectives of different groups within the organization. In other words, it might state the development plan for managers, outline the development plan for employees, list the courses and/or experiences that will help each group reach their training goals, and finally show how trainees will move through the training process and under what timelines. The plan should also clearly indicate how the trainees will know that they have successfully completed the training and specify the recognition that they will receive as a result, whether financial, in title, or both.

As examined in chapter 2, successful organizations will recognize this link between strategic human resource development and strategic business goals and use this link to gain a competitive advantage. In other words, trainers must "run training like a business" and achieve effectiveness by linking the training to business strategy, focusing less on content and more on the business issues, being more responsive to customers, and remembering the department's business mission (van Adelsberg & Trolley, 1999). Without this strategic sense of self, the training department risks ineffectiveness at best and floundering at worst.

Strategic Training Requires Leadership

The training department must have a leader who fills the role of strategist and builds the relationships within the organization that provide the link between strategic planning and reality. One organization with which I am familiar has a training plan aligned with company strategy. In fact, the company strategy and the training plan are driven by business objectives. Recently, the training manager left to join another company. While the training department staff members wait for a replacement manager, they are "on hold," lacking direction, dropping classes, and losing support within the organization for the classes left on the calendar. The new training manager will have to build momentum once again, and reestablish the relationships with top managers and line managers to ensure that training is important and helpful to them in reaching their goals. The good news, however, is that in the interim, the trainers are learning to take on the role of strategists themselves and working to build relationships and to market their services so that the department does not lose too much momentum.

Listening to internal customers and building relationships with them is critically important for trainers to achieve impact in the modern workplace. Trainers must be sure to attend department meetings so that they can keep their finger on the pulse of the organization and build the necessary trust with the line level managers (Dust, 1996). The relationships trainers have with the managers within the company will be built over time and require great diligence on the trainers' part. Trainers frequently need to educate others and to market their services to develop trust in the training organization. Whether the trainers are internal or external to the organization, they will need to have buy-in at all levels to succeed in reaching the goals, which requires constant work and marketing (Dust, 1996) as detailed later in this chapter.

To help ensure that trainers are effectively wearing the strategist hat, a training group can use the checklist in table 7.1 at least once a year. By following these guidelines, trainers will attempt to ensure that departmental actions are strategically aligned with organizational objectives and work to better meet customer needs.

THE TRAINER AS ANALYST

The second traditional role of the trainer is that of *analyst*. The trainer in today's workplace must be competent with all facets of analysis involved in training—conducting performance and training assessments, evaluating results after training, and calculating the organization's return on investment. Needs assessment is discussed in detail in chapter 3, so it will not be explicated at length here.

An important next step for a trainer, after determining strategy, is to find out what real needs exist in the organization and whether training can or cannot meet these needs. If the department cannot meet a certain need, the trainer must be able to analyze the *performance* issue and determine what intervention would be appropriate to recommend, whether it be process improvement, organizational change, improved recognition systems, or simple team building, and so on. Again, this role (that is, to be able to analyze situations and make recommendations) underlines the importance of trainers staying abreast of current issues and trends and knowing what resources are available. Networking, cross-training, researching new ideas,

Table 7.1
Checklist for Strategist Role

√ Begin the year with a frank discussion with the top leader of the organization. Find out what the current business strategy for success is—the company strengths, the company weaknesses, and the plan for addressing each. Ask how the leader sees the role of training and development in helping to achieve the goals and what you can do better to improve service to the company.

√ Meet individually with departmental leaders and ask them what they see as their department's strategy for success and how that aligns with the overall goals. Ask what they see as the role of training and development in helping to achieve their goals and what you can do better to improve service to their department.

√ Meet with focus groups of employees and ask them what they see as their individual strategies for success in their position and how that aligns with both the goals of the department and the overall goals of the company. Ask them what the training department can do better to improve service to them individually.

√ Meet as a department to discuss your findings, create annual goals, and determine how these goals will support the larger goals of the organization.

√ Make sure trainers are present at relevant meetings so that the department can keep a finger on what is happening within the organization.

√ Benchmark with other trainers (both in and out of the industry) to compare the department's strategic direction, along with strategic techniques others are using.

√ Publish the department's goals; ask for feedback from all stakeholders and incorporate.

implementing projects, and exercising responsibility all enable the trainer to maintain a vital role in the organization.

Evaluating the results of training is also a task frequently neglected by trainers, even though the methods of evaluation are known (Kirkpatrick, 1996). The problem is that often trainers don't assess programs beyond the reaction level of evaluation. Indeed, research indicates that the most commonly assessed training outcome is trainees' affective reactions (Frazis, Herz, & Horrigan, 1995). From a strategic standpoint, it is important for trainers to recognize that if they wish to prove their business case for providing programs offered through the training plan, they may need to verify effectiveness with supporting data. Trainers should report that data in a convincing format so that the rest of the organization can easily comprehend and appreciate the value of their work.

In many training programs, testing can be useful to show positive results. However, it is not sufficient to simply demonstrate that learning has taken place. Further testing, or perhaps even follow-up one-on-one assessment, can be used to examine whether training is being used on the job although it may not definitively prove that positive transfer prevailed. And the fear around testing may have a negative impact on employees.

Therefore, qualitative data can be useful for trainers to collect and analyze. By gathering and publishing positive trainee feedback that can be found on course evaluation forms, trainers may be able to gain better support and achieve greater turnout for future classes. Furthermore, when positive messages about the workshops are published via e-mail or in a training newsletter, managers are more likely to send people to future workshops.

Trainers can also collect, analyze, and publish positive customer service comments from employees and customers, possibly by linking training with companywide recognition efforts. By honoring employees who are using the skills featured in the commentaries, the company is more likely to reinforce the desired behaviors. Indeed, social learning theory (Bandura, 1986) indicates that people will imitate the behavior of credible people who are rewarded for their positive behavior. Tracking customer satisfaction rates and linking them to specific skills taught in the workshop can also help to monitor the impact of training and help market it within the company. For example, if service recovery is a skill being taught in a customer service workshop, tracking rates of successful recovery with customers will help to bolster the case for training on that skill and encourage greater use of the skill by other employees.

Moreover, trainers should create and administer their own customer satisfaction surveys and analyze the results. Training personnel can track which departments feel that they have gotten the best support from training, how easy or difficult it is for employees to register for classes, how relevant the class offerings have been to address the current employee and department needs, and so on.

And finally, it is important for trainers to analyze and evaluate financial data about the training department. Trainers can assess how well the budget is meeting current needs, what the return on investment is, and what adjustments need to be made in future years. Again, methods for doing this are known (for example, Carnevale & Schulz, 1990; Parry, 1996); the problem is that trainers sometimes avoid using them. Research has shown that results outcomes are used by less than 50 percent of companies conducting training evaluations (Frazis et al., 1995). Some may not make time to address the financial issues on a strategic level. Nonetheless, the role of the trainer as strategic analyst, like the role of marketing analyst, is critical if trainers want to ensure the greatest impact for their work.

An Illustration: Trainer as Strategic Analyst

For example, at one company, we strategically linked the desired customer service skills learned in a training program to a reward and recognition system that used, among other things, positive storytelling to reinforce the behavior. The system provided a way for peers to recognize outstanding acts of service among themselves, as well as a method for noting and analyzing exceptional external service. Built around the theme of sports teams, the internal recognition tool was called Player's Choice Award, and the external tool was called a Most Valuable Player Award. When a worker was recognized internally, the story about the service was posted on a large bulletin board in the cafeteria with copies going to the department manager and to the recipient's personnel file.

Furthermore, if a letter was received from an external client, it was written up on the MVP Award form and also posted. Employees could read the stories about each other on the board and share in the positive feelings. Employees who received the most awards were invited to an annual recognition banquet, and the best of the stories were told to the gathered audience so that positive reinforcement was given to recipients in front of their peers. This encouraged others to deliver a high level of service as well. The program has been very popular and has helped to ensure people are rewarded for the trained skills they have demonstrated in the workplace and that the company wants repeated.

THE TRAINER AS INSTRUCTIONAL DESIGNER

Another traditional role of the trainer is that of *instructional designer*. The critical question in this section is, what can trainers do to achieve even higher standards for their training design efforts? In today's workplace, trainers can use instructional design to greatly enhance the classroom and the on-the-job experience of the employee. When done well, properly designed and packaged training can enhance learning, increase relevance, and ensure greater understanding. It can create an indelible experience for trainees and send a subtle message that they are important enough to be given high-quality training.

However, because many trainers possess limited knowledge of adult learning theory (Caudron, 2000), they may lack specific skills in designing training for maximum learning. They may design their own course material and present the material somewhat spontaneously, based on a brief outline. For some, this works well—they have enough talent as a presenter to carry it off. For others, however, presentations may be inconsistent from class to class, since other trainers will not be able to present that particular training session as well as a more skilled presenter. Naturally, when this divergence occurs, the impact of the training is weakened because participants may not be effectively exposed to all the key concepts. Moreover, the perceived quality of the program may suffer as participants can usually tell when the presentation is ad lib and ill-prepared.

On the other hand, some trainers are very conscientious about presenting consistently, but their workshops do not achieve high impact because the material is not put together using accepted principles of instructional design based on adult learning methods (for an extended discussion, see chapter 5). For example, too often employees are subjected to lecture-style sessions in formalized classroom settings because the trainer has not been able to design pieces of the program that will make it hands-on, interactive, and experiential—an essential ingredient for training success (Pike, 1994).

Then again, there are many trainers who present consistently and inspirationally using appropriate design principles, but their materials lack the packaging and branding that imbue the workshop with a valuable and enduring quality for the employees. Material may be creative but hastily stapled together, or printed only in black-and-white, or filled with poorly designed pages with either too much or not enough text. Unfortunately, this underwhelming approach can undermine trainers' credibility, even if participants don't actually express their complaints. Just as a salesperson is mindful of maximizing the sale by polishing his/her presentation, material, and personal appearance, the trainer should convey the same polish and attention to detail.

Finally, training materials are oftentimes unrelated to other training programs or the corporate identity, making programs appear isolated and not connected to the overall strategic plan of the training department or the organization as a whole. On the one hand, trainers may not want to dwindle training dollars on purchasing color materials or using a graphic artist to package the materials. They may want to focus more on the "steak" than the "sizzle" (as stated by one of my clients). Yet, if trainers want not only to meet, but also to exceed, customer expectations, they should consider branding and packaging as refinements to add value to products and services.

Simple solutions to design issues exist if trainers want to raise the bar on their own performance in this area. First of all, trainers should consider attending a comprehensive workshop on instructional design as part of their professional development plan. Many such workshops are available and, of course, there are many books available for self-study. However, a workshop where trainers can "learn by doing" is probably more effective. If a trainer is a one-person training department or consulting service, design knowledge will be especially important. If a trainer is part of a multiperson training department, one person may be selected to be the design specialist and act as the internal expert. Then, appropriate instructor guides can be constructed for all programs using applicable basic standards, so that consistency is improved.

Additionally, this formal construction of instructor guides and corresponding participant workbooks will encourage trainers to incorporate a variety of activities that appeal to different learning styles and to use specific learning models that encourage training transfer. For example, in be-havior-change programs, it is important to consider how trainers will model the behaviors they want employees to use. The use of video is very effective, but, if it is not available, trainers can use prewritten scenarios to be read aloud by volunteer participants. To reiterate, by creating instructionally sound materials, trainers will create a more interactive, high-quality, well-planned learning experience for participants.

An important point should be made regarding web-based or com-puter-based training. Trainers who are designing programs to be used on-line should beware of these same pitfalls. Content that is hastily put together and lacks instructional depth and quality is just as ineffective on-line as it is on paper.

As for packaging and branding, trainers can easily improve the quality of their materials, making them more noteworthy, by asking for help from the marketing department or from internal or external graphic design re-sources. More on this topic will be presented later in this chapter under in-ternal marketing. However, the key point is that if trainers pay attention to participants' perception of materials and to the total training package, they will enhance the credibility of the department, the value of the materials, and the appreciation of the quality of the material by the participants.

THE TRAINER AS FACILITATOR

Another traditional role of the trainer is that of *facilitator*. Much has been written in the popular literature on this topic, particularly about the art of training (for example, how to avoid stage fright, how to prepare for a pre-sentation, how to engage the learner through interaction, and so on). Most high-impact trainers are aware of the importance of acknowledging adult learning styles and using the "Aha!" discovery process to "facilitate" adult learning, rather than just lecturing. And many trainers are learning to use web-based training and other interactive training methods, rather than simply relying on one-way lecture sessions.

This lecture approach no longer meets customer expectations. Audi-ences expect to be entertained, and trainers must recognize the importance of the idea of "entertrainment" (Walter, 1995). Skilled trainers have always recognized the importance of entertaining their audiences, consequently striving to put on a good performance. They've always known the value of telling an interesting story or using a clever joke as an illustration. They've often incorporated business games into their presentations to create "expe-riential" learning. And many have used creative training methods to in-crease the value and quality of their programs.

However, again the bar has been raised. To compete, trainers must im-prove their training techniques, and consider turning every workshop into full-fledged, theater-style entertainment experiences. This can be done on different levels—not every "show" requires high-end audiovisual equipment—but should always be done in a way that exceeds expectations and is as innovative as possible. This means attention to detail. Trainers can raise their performance levels by paying attention to the "props," such as four-color workbooks (wrapped and tied with string), or the food (themed to tie into the training concept), or room decorations, or a special audio-visual presentation.

Trainers also must hone their performance and enhance it through development of a "stage persona," so they can influence participants on a variety of emotional and intellectual levels (Dowling, 1995). It means becoming a master storyteller and using anecdotes to truly enrich the learning experience. It means augmenting the training ritual through food, lighting, music, and personal reflection.

On the other hand, high-impact trainers should never cross the line into manipulation of emotions. Further, they should not use fancy materials to cover up weaknesses in basic instructional design. The goal is merely to modify a good program and make it outstanding through more effective packaging and attention to detail.

Effective Facilitation: An Illustration

At a marketing company several years back, we used a "Disney-type approach" to create a comprehensive performance experience for participants called the Journey. Working with a team of creative design professionals, we used many innovative techniques to engage the learner and create an extraordinary learning experience. Designed to train certain employees to become the "cultural ambassadors" of the organization and facilitate the cultural development of the company, the Journey was themed around the tribal concept. It took participants on a journey from past to present to help them understand the business enterprise as a social system and the role of a corporate culture within that society.

Each element of the training was carefully themed and packaged, from the brown-paper-wrapped participant workbooks designed by our artists, to the "trail mix" served to the "travelers," to the themed room décor and tribal artifacts placed around the room. Special lighting and music were chosen to reinforce each theme developed in the six-day program and created an atmosphere of awe and wonder for participants as they walked into the room on the first day. Thus, through attention to detail and "the show," we were able to engage the learners more fully and to create a powerful learning experience.

THE TRAINER AS ADMINISTRATOR

The next traditional role of the trainer is that of *administrator*. Generally speaking, the administrator role of a trainer is looked down upon because it is not one of his/her more glamorous and creative roles. However, the skill with which the trainer administers the process logistically can be as important to the success of the training as being present in the room and delivering an effective workshop. Administrative details such as how the room appears to students when they enter, whether the session begins and ends on time, how the training materials are presented, and even whether or not food is served—all can leave a lasting impression on a student.

Administration of a training event should begin long before the actual training date. First of all, the trainer must be entirely aware of what material will be presented during the course by means of either a well-thought-out instructor guide or a detailed outline. The trainer and the (internal or external) client have agreed upon the content of the workshop. Goals of the training should be clearly established and expectations of results predetermined. If this is the first time the workshop is presented, the trainer should have some practice run-throughs with fellow trainers or pilot groups to elicit feedback and to work through problem areas of the training. This is also an excellent opportunity to learn the material so that the trainer will be able to focus on the students rather than on the material during the presentation.

Depending upon the length of the training program, the dates and times of the training event need to be coordinated with the participating departments to ensure the maximum number of participants. Involving a department manager or spokesperson in this process is extremely helpful in order to make him/her responsible for ensuring employees' attendance. As much as possible, trainers should let the department managers decide when the training should be held and manage the task of scheduling people. Trainers should be sure to provide time slots for training on all shifts, if possible, so that no participant is unreasonably inconvenienced. This also demonstrates the customer-focus of the training department and can help a great deal to establish positive relationships with line managers and employees.

A standard, customer-focused procedure for signup should be put in place to make it easy for students to enroll in classes. Even if trainers are not directly involved with the signup of students, they should be aware of who and how many will be attending the classes. This is because no trainer likes to wait in an empty room expecting students to arrive, only to find that several people have cancelled or rescheduled. To increase interest on the part of the participants, the training department should send letters of invitation to prospective attendees, explaining the goals of the program and what they will be expected to do during the session. Prework assignments can be included in the invitation. After participants are registered, a confirmation letter should be sent, detailing when and where the class will be held. These are techniques that have long been used by external training firms, but they are often not used as frequently internally. While the process can be time-consuming, if systems are set up to automatically produce the confirmation letters, the process is easier. The purpose is not only to avoid confusion over who will be attending, but also to start the experience of the participants on a positive note.

When the first day of training arrives, it is important for the trainer to assume the role of host in the training room as if inviting a group of people into his/her home. As will be discussed later in this chapter, the training event is a corporate ritual that can be greatly enhanced by the appropriate preparation of the training room. The training program also can approximate a theatrical event—or at least should be perceived that way. The stage should be properly set, with all the props in place, for maximum impact when trainees enter. Even if the training "event" is a computer-based training session, the student's experience should be made entertaining, engaging, and carefully staged for maximum impact. Indeed, gaining the attention of learners is the first step toward increasing their motivation (Keller, 1984).

To fully engage the audience, trainers should greet the trainees at the door, begin the session on time, have scheduled breaks, and end the training when expected. These are basic Training 101 principles, but they require diligent and effective administration to ensure that they are followed in the increasingly rushed and chaotic workplace. Trainers should also do the following:

1. Make sure that they have adequate technology to support training administration, whether online or in the classroom.
2. Distribute and track evaluations that include both qualitative and quantitative data so that they can later be used for internal marketing.
3. Keep accurate records of employee participation. (This may not be the most enjoyable or glamorous task of a trainer, but it is important to trainees and it helps to encourage participation in follow-up sessions. Moreover, participation records can be used to affirm the value of the training and its link to the strategic business goals.)

As part of the administration function, trainers are additionally responsible for accurately tracking how the training program has affected employees in their work environment and determining how well they have put the information to use. A variety of techniques for tracking transfer of training are available—the problem is that too many organizational trainers lack the interest, discipline, and support to implement them. To raise training to a new level, trainers will want to become more skilled in these methods and carefully track results and activities that support the overall training effort. (For more details on training transfer, please revisit chapter 5.)

THE NEW ROLES OF TRAINERS

At the beginning of this chapter, several new roles for trainers were identified. The next part of this chapter will focus on what appears to be the primary new roles of trainers, as based in the literature (for example, Bachler, 1997; Galagan & Salopek, 2000) and my personal experience. These three new roles are change ambassador, marketer, and spiritual leader. Each role is discussed in turn.

THE TRAINER AS CHANGE AMBASSADOR

The first of the new roles of trainers to be discussed is that of *change ambassador*. As a consequence of the exponential rate of change in our business world, many employees are afflicted with fear because of the uncertainty they sense in their work environment. And because trainers are usually the ones who teach the new operating methods, they are increasingly the ones who must reassure the employees and encourage employees to see the benefits of the changes. Trainers themselves must become "ambassadors of change" (Fryer, 1999), smoothing the way for employees to incorporate new methodologies.

What can trainers do to become effective ambassadors of change? First and foremost, they must understand that resistance to change is inherent in human nature. They must recognize that not only are employees coping with their feelings about change, but trainers are also dealing with their own feelings about change. Therefore, trainers must consciously strive to overcome the resistance in themselves, whether it's because they are having to expand their roles within the organization or because, like most people, they just do not like change, period. In spite of this, it is important for trainers to embrace change and welcome it (Mager, 1996). After all, trainers have always urged their training participants to accept change and to modify their behavior by the way they think about and perform their jobs. Today, the initiatives are merely on a larger scale, from simply changing to a customer-focused environment, for example, to changing an entire work process.

The second thing trainers must do to become effective ambassadors of change is to recognize the importance of their role in the process in order to help people implement change in a positive manner. They can use their influence to overcome resistance, manage the transition, shape political dynamics, and help workers understand new tasks (Noe, 1999). To help overcome resistance, trainers should be willing listeners, empathizing with employees who are dealing with the change. They should also use and teach techniques that will involve employees in planning and implementing the changes, so that employees have more buy-in and will be able to understand how the change will improve their performance and better meet their needs.

To help manage the transition, trainers should facilitate communicating the goals and vision of an organizational initiative, so that employees can understand that positive results will come out of the changes and maintain a positive attitude. During this transition period, the role of change agent can meld with that of spiritual leader as trainers try to help people to "keep the faith" and not lose sight of the overall value of the project and the work they are doing. The role of change ambassador also melds with that of marketer during the change transition period as trainers learn to use formal and informal communication techniques to help market the change effort and keep the change momentum going.

Trainers may be able to influence the political dynamics of change by working closely with the management team to achieve their organizational and departmental goals. They should work on building relationships with the managers, approaching their needs in a customer-focused manner to show them how training can aid them in their efforts. Trainers must make sure that the training department adds value to the business and that they are building their credibility within the management team (Laabs, 1995). They can also build these relationships with employees and show them how the tools that are being taught and how the changes that are being implemented will help them meet their own individual development needs. And, of course, trainers must use training to help both managers and employees learn how to do their job under new work models and to use the new tools and techniques to complete their work effectively. Table 7.2 outlines important summary points about the change ambassador role.

An Example of Facilitating Change in Organizational Development

One company with which I am familiar has been recently immersed in a major organizational transformation effort. Initially, we were brought in to determine what training might be needed in order to help employees perform more effectively as part of the large-scale marketing overhaul. However, it soon became obvious that there were major organizational issues within the company, as a consequence of a recent merger and unsettling senior management turnover. Soon after two focus groups were facilitated, it became clear that training was not necessarily appropriate at this point in the company's journey as there were many deeper issues to be addressed in order to improve the company's performance, both financially and culturally.

Upon conducting a needs assessment, I recommended a number of interventions to address the organizational needs, including a management development initiative, a process improvement initiative, and a cultural initiative that combined improved training, communication, and merger activities. A team of experts was brought in to assist with the process, in-

Table 7.2
Checklist for Change Ambassador Role

√ Be open to change yourself.

√ Educate yourself on change management and performance improvement.

√ Educate managers on change management and performance improvement.

√ Bring in change and/or process improvement experts before implementing large changes.

√ Build positive relationships with managers and employees.

√ Ensure the training department is customer focused.

√ Ensure training is linked to business strategy.

√ Improve your social skills to maximize your ability to influence others when important.

√ Build the credibility of the training department.

√ Use careful and thoughtful planning processes to help manage the change effort.

√ Work as a united team both inside and outside the department to determine the best ways to address change.

√ Recognize and acknowledge human issues when dealing with employees and managers.

√ Help create and communicate a positive vision.

√ Analyze if training will be needed to meet the changing business environment.

√ Learn about and consider other holistic performance interventions to recommend, beyond formal classroom training.

cluding an executive coach, a process improvement specialist, and other training and development specialists as needed. A team of graphic designers, marketing specialists, and an interior designer worked to redesign those systems to ensure a consistent approach in all of our efforts. In other words, we did not try to apply training as a solution for the entire company, but rather used a multidimensional approach to move toward the vision of a unified, high-performing organization.

THE TRAINER AS MARKETER

The second of the new roles of trainers is that of a marketer. In an era of information overload and increasing competition for the attention of employees, trainers are finding it necessary to market the training department inside the organization to gain buy-in and participation (Dust, 1996; Laabs, 1995). This is one aspect of marketing that is important for trainers to recognize and master. However, a second aspect of marketing that is important to distinguish is using training to "advertise" the company, its goals, and its corporate culture to employees.

Marketing Training to the Organization

First, it is important for trainers to learn how to market their services to the rest of the organization. Initially, it is important to publicize upcoming classes and activities to ensure greater awareness of the products and services available to employees and managers. This assures that participation levels are good. Second, it is important to publish feedback on the workshops. This assures that managers and employees recognize the value of workshops. Third, trainers should market the credibility of the training department by establishing relationships with top management, line managers, and employee groups. This assures that the organization wants to return to the training department for help in reaching performance goals.

In order to market more effectively, high-impact trainers can take lessons from the marketing world and use those techniques to help in their marketing efforts. In marketing, *image* and *identity* are key words. All information sends messages about the image and identity of a particular product. Likewise, in every piece of training communication, trainers make a statement about the image of the department (which speaks to credibility) and the identity of the department (which speaks to the type of service one can expect from the department).

As claimed by Dust (1996), image matters. Therefore, when creating and producing material for training, consider each item a marketing device, from the cover of the participants' workbooks, to the slides, to the web site, to the logo representing the corporate university. The "training brand" presents a particular image and identity that is consistent with the goals of the department. Each collateral training item should enhance the credibility of the program and the department. And each item should make the material inviting and notable to the participant. In other words, the branding and packaging of the training can influence transfer of training.

Marketing Training Programs: An Example

When possible, a program can be tied to an overall brand for the company or the department, so that all training programs are perceived as part of the "brand" package. For example, at one company, the service culture and business strategy is based on a customer service program called FOCUS. Accordingly, when designing a follow-on program for a specific department that needed on-the-job training modules, the program was tied into the FOCUS brand and was called FOCUS on Performance: For Cashiers. Key themes from the customer service training were repeated and underlined in the content of the on-the-job training program. Further, key packaging themes were repeated (for example, the same color scheme and type style were used in the follow-on program, along with a professionally designed color cover and spine for the participant binder). As a result, employees were better able to link the customer service training to the on-the-job training and to apply the skills in their operations. The repetition in the theme, content, and packaging of the program helped to enhance their transfer of learning. The training department also validated its credibility by responding to line-level needs with a high-quality product that was tied to the strategic direction of the company.

Marketing the Organization and Its Goals

The marketing concept can be extended even further. Another name for internal marketing might be "employee communication," but there is more to it than that. Marketing—if employed appropriately—is a tool that can be used by the company to "brand" and "advertise" its vision, mission, values, and goals, to help garner employee support. The word *appropriate* is important. It is not appropriate to attempt to brainwash employees. It is appropriate to communicate a belief system to them that they are free to choose to accept or not.

For example, a company orientation program is an important means to communicate the corporate culture. It is a rite of passage that initiates the new employee into the "tribe." Handled well, the orientation "markets" the company to the employees and validates their decision to join. It helps to create a sense of purpose and belonging in the new employees, and it speaks to the quality of the organization, its "image," and "identity."

In this light, any training program (especially behavior-change training) can be seen as an internal marketing event in which employees are asked to believe that a certain new way of behaving is better than the old way. Using expertise, logic, and the power of influence, trainers encourage participants to buy their product (that is, to buy into behaving in a new or different way).

When training initiatives are linked to planned communication (that is, marketing) activities, the impact of training is reinforced. Marketing provides a systematic method of communicating the cultural messages and using them to gain continued buy-in, whether through training and awareness events, newsletters, signage, or participant materials. Trainers can work with organizational leaders to develop and execute a series of planned communication activities that bolster training goals and maintain learning transfer. For example, a workshop could be followed by a series of planned brown-bag lunches or refresher meetings to reinforce the training skills or messages. In sum, it is important for high-impact trainers to recognize that marketing supports their work and to use it to expand their realm of influence—when appropriate—to strengthen the organization's culture and link training initiatives to organizational goals.

A Marketing Success Story

For one large start-up organization in Detroit, my firm was part of a consulting team assembled to implement an internal marketing initiative. The object was to develop a positive corporate culture from the beginning by using a variety of communication, training, and team-building activities to support the organizational cultural goals. The first step was to create an internal logo, Motor City Drive: Fueled by Fun, Powered by Pride. This logo represented the internal values of the company and was used as a launching point to tie together an entire system of cultural communication pieces.

All cultural "touchpoints" were managed through this process, from the recruiting and prehire process to the orientation and training, through the operational training. Each item in the process was examined for cultural continuity, and all elements were designed to be consistent and to reinforce the internal brand. The orientation was called the Key (to Motor City), the employee handbook was called *The Road Map*, and the operations manuals were called *The Travel Guides*. An employee kick-off event was also tied to the brand concept. Each cultural element was tied together visually and thematically, thereby reinforcing the values. Partially as a result of this work, the service culture within the company was quickly established and has remained strong since opening day. This approach has increased both employee and customer retention. At a minimum, the cultural development activities sent a very strong message to every employee that they were valued and that the company was willing to invest time and money to get that message across.

THE TRAINER AS SPIRITUAL LEADER

One of the most interesting new roles of today's trainers, but perhaps the least recognized, is that of spiritual leader. In the contemporary business environment, trainers are increasingly dealing with participants who are discouraged, cynical, fearful, and doubtful about their work (Fryer, 1999; Kuczmarski & Kuczmarski, 1995). Having dealt with enormous changes in the business world and what seems to be an unchecked drive for the almighty dollar, many employees feel they have lost control over their daily work lives and are losing hope that the situation will improve. Many feel that their jobs have become meaningless and void of purpose (Terez, 2000). They have become as spiritually bereft as the organizations they work for. Simply put, many employees have lost their faith.

As a result, trainees often come to training sessions discouraged, ready to gripe if they still have the energy, or worse, just sit there passively, too dispirited to participate. Whether they realize it or not, when they attend training sessions they are often seeking the encouragement and inspiration they need to continue the struggle and to find meaning and higher purpose again in their daily work lives. They are looking for someone who can heal their work wounds and give them faith in the working world.

Given this malaise, we can better understand why a session called Faith at Work led by Ken Blanchard and Bob Pike at the ASTD Conference 2000, was filled to overflowing. "It sounds like a revival in here," commented Pike. And in truth, it was! Although many participants were there to learn how their training work was connected to their religious beliefs, what they perhaps didn't realize was that they, too, were there for their own "spiritual healing" and "revival." They were seeking renewal from their own spiritual leaders, Blanchard and Pike, who use such events to provide the inspiration trainers and leaders need in the workplace to continue their search for meaning and purpose in their own lives. And Blanchard and Pike (who received a divinity degree from the Moody Bible Institute in Chicago) clearly show the link between ministering to the spiritually bereft inside the church and ministering to the spiritually bereft within the workplace. They are living examples of how many of the techniques used by ministers, rabbis, priests, and even the shaman to sustain and restore the spiritually deprived outside the workplace are also successful if used (appropriately) inside the workplace.

For example, storytelling is one of the most powerful techniques used by religious leaders to teach desired behaviors in the outside world. Storytelling has also been recognized for its powerful role in fostering and maintaining organizational cultures (Daft, 2001). As such, to communicate and teach desired behaviors inside organizations, trainers can use this same technique very effectively. Blanchard and Pike are two of the masters of this storytelling approach. But other "pastoral" techniques are essential in the trainer's world as well, such as empathetic listening, problem solving, advising, guiding, community building, and inspiring (Hequet, 1995).

There are even more parallels with ministry—workshops must be prepared and presented effectively, just as sermons must be prepared and presented effectively. In both professional roles there is ritual management —creating a time and a place that enables participants to more fully engage in their spiritual development through music, lighting, rituals, environment, and human interaction. And both professions are responsible for teaching—through thoughtful and inspirational messages, participants in both the classroom and the church or synagogue get spiritual replenishment and are more willing and able to take on the outside world once again. The most engaging of these spiritual trainers know how to entertain as well as to inspire in their presentations, so that the experience can be heightened for participants and create a lasting impression that will manifest itself in their daily lives.

All this is not to say that trainers should advocate their personal religious beliefs in the classroom or that they should ever cross the line into emotional manipulation that does not allow participants to choose their own actions and beliefs. Consequently, the role of spiritual leader must be handled very carefully and responsibly. But if trainers better understand their "workplace spirit" role, and the needs and expectations that participants may bring to their sessions, they can more effectively use their skills, enthusiasm, and influence to help bring about positive changes in the workplace.

A HISTORICAL PERSPECTIVE FOR SPIRITUALITY IN THE WORKPLACE

Let us explore this idea of spirituality in the workplace in some greater depth. The nineteenth-century anthropologist Émile Durkeim pointed out that in the industrial age many of the tribal and family bonds that had sustained humanity for millions of years were being destroyed. In 1893 Durkeim noted in his book *The Division of Labor in Society* that as modern society evolved, the "ties" that bound people to their families, communities, and traditions were being loosened. As a result of this disconnection, he felt that there was increased "anomie," or alienation, in society as well as in the workplace. Due to the sheer numbers of people in cities, he saw that people were increasingly isolated and alienated from each other and lacking in shared beliefs, rituals, and values. Further, because people were spending more time at work and less time with their families, people were not participating in the daily rituals and traditions and relationships that had provided meaning and fulfillment in the past. And last, at a time when assembly line work was becoming increasingly dominant, with higher specialization of trades and work skills, people were becoming more isolated from each other even on the job.

Durkeim noted an increase in crime and suicide as a result of these factors and warned that these issues must be addressed or would result in great social upheaval. He suggested that corporations had a role and a responsibility in addressing the situation, or they would suffer adverse consequences. This sentiment was echoed by Susan and Thomas Kuczmarski, authors of *Values-Based Leadership* (1995), who noted three forms of anomie in the contemporary world: societal, individual, and corporate. They wrote that today's workplaces are filled with people who are demoralized by the uncertainty around them and who don't believe in their work or organizations anymore. Fulfillment and satisfaction from work, they claim, is diminishing.

In his book *The Human Zoo*, anthropologist Desmond Morris (1969) points out that, in order to cope with such strains and disconnection of modern society, humans have created personal tribes, using their network of family and associates, who provide them with the connections they need to sustain them in their hectic worlds. Morris has used the phone book of Los Angeles as an example of a "supertribe" we have created to help us structure and make sense out of society and a personal address book as the symbol of our "personal" tribes.

Similarly, it could be argued that the corporate telephone directory has become a symbol of our "work" tribe, and we become members of our corporate tribes. With that perspective, corporate culture takes on a whole new meaning, and we see the work tribe as a society unto itself, with its own culture, artifacts, rituals, mythology, and hierarchy. As an example, Morris shows how certain corporate activities, such as orientations, are actually a kind of tribal ritual, similar to rites of passage rituals. It is important to note that rites of passage rituals have also been examined in the literature about organizational cultures (Trice & Beyer, 1984).

If the corporation is a tribe, then it could be argued that the trainer is the "shaman" of the tribe—a spiritual healer who provides healing and rejuvenation to the soul of the corporate employee. Consider the words of anthropologist Dr. Michael Harner (1980) in his book *The Way of the Shaman*:

Shamans . . . are the keepers of a remarkable body of ancient techniques that they use to achieve and maintain well-being and healing for themselves and members of their communities. . . . Shamanism is a great mental and emotional adventure, one in which the patient as well as the shaman-healer are involved. Through his heroic journey and efforts, the shaman helps his patients transcend their normal, ordinary definition of reality, including the definition of themselves as ill. The shaman shows his patients that they are not emotionally and spiritually alone in their struggles against illness and death. The shaman shares his special powers and convinces his patients, on a deep level of consciousness, that another human is willing to offer up his own self to help them. The shaman's self-sacrifice calls forth a commensurate emotional commitment from his patients, a sense of obligation to struggle alongside the shaman to save one's self. Caring and curing go hand in hand. (p. xvii)

If the word *trainer* is substituted for the word *shaman* in this caption, the description might accurately describe the world of today's inspired trainers, who are passionate about their work and their desire to help their participants. In this context, the trainer becomes much more than "task trainer," more than "teacher," more than "strategist," and even more than "consultant." As such, trainers are not only ambassadors of change, but also ambassadors of the corporate culture. Their role is to guide people along in their personal and professional journey, to help them grow mentally and spiritually, and to help them rediscover a sense of purpose and meaning at work.

This responsibility, of course, can be extremely draining for trainers as they cope with the struggles of so many people within their workplaces. It takes an emotional toll, which may cause some trainers to eventually burn out or to seek a change in their career or their company to relieve the strain. On the other hand, like ministers who are "called" to their work, many trainers feel called to their profession and find it difficult to let go. Their work provides their own sense of purpose and meaning and must be conducted to sustain their emotional, mental, and spiritual satisfaction.

CONCLUSION

It is this kind of passion and love for the work and the people who inspire trainers to go on, despite the obstacles and the setbacks, and to continue their professional journey—even when it "sacrifices the self"—in order to help fulfill the dreams of those around them. Those are the trainers who achieve great impact in the workplace—trainers who are not only competent in their traditional roles, but also in their new, less clearly defined, yet vitally important roles of change ambassador, marketer, and spiritual leader.

BIBLIOGRAPHY

Bachler, C.J. (1997, June). The trainer's role is turning upside down. *Workforce*, pp. 93–105.

Bandura, A. (1986). *Social foundations of thought and action: A social cognitive theory*. Englewood Cliffs, NJ: Prentice Hall.

Carnavale, A.P., & Schulz, E.R. (1990). Return on investment: Accounting for training. *Training and Development Journal, 7*, S1:S32.

Caudron, S. (2000). Learners speak out. *Training and Development Journal, 54(4)*, 52–57.

Daft, R.L. (2001). *Organization theory and design*. (7th ed.). Cincinnati, OH: Southwestern.

Dowling, E. (1995). *The standup trainer: Techniques from the theater and the comedy club to help your students laugh, stay awake, and learn something useful*. Alexandria, VA: American Society for Training and Development.

Durkheim, É. (1893). *The division of labor in society*. Paris: Alcan. Tr.

Dust, B. (1996). Marketing training services internally. *Training and Development Journal, 50(10)*, 60.

Frazis, H.J., Herz, D.E., & Horrigan, M.W. (1995). Employer-provided training: Results from a new survey. *Monthly Labor Review, 118*, 3–17.

Fryer, B. (1999, July). Ambassadors of change. *Inside Technology Training*, 18–22.

Galagan, P.A., & Salopek, J.J. (2000). Training's new guard. *Training and Development Journal, 54(5)*, 34–55.

Harner, M. (1980). *The way of the shaman*. New York, NY: Harper Collins Publishers.

Hequet, M. (1995, December). The new trainer. *Training Magazine*, 23–29.

Keller, J.M. (1984). The use of the ARCS model of motivation in teacher training. In K. Shaw (Ed.), *Aspects of Educational Technology (Vol. XVII)* (pp. 289–320). London: Kogan Page.

Kirkpatrick, D.L. (1996). Evaluation. (2nd ed.). In R.L. Craig (Ed.), *The ASTD Training and Development Handbook* (pp. 294–312). New York: McGraw Hill.

Kuczmarski, S., & Kuczmarski, T. (1995). *Values-based leadership*. Englewood Cliffs, NJ: Prentice Hall.

Laabs, J.J. (1995). Put your job on the line. *Personnel Journal, 74(6)*, 74–88.

Mager, R.F. (1996, June). Morphing into a 21st century trainer. *Training Magazine*, 47–54.

Martocchio, J.J., & Baldwin, T.T. (1997). The evolution of strategic organizational training. In G.R. Ferris (Ed.), *Research in Personnel and Human Resource Management* (pp. 1–46). Greenwich, CT: JAI Press.

Morris, D. (1969). *The human zoo.* Tokyo: Kodansha International.

Noe, R.A. (1999). *Employee training and development.* Boston: Irwin McGraw-Hill.

Parry, S.D. (1996). Measuring training's ROI. *Training and Development Journal, 5,* 72–77.

Pike, R.W. (1994). *Creative training techniques handbook.* Minneapolis, MN: Lakewood Books.

Terez, T. (2000). *22 keys to creating a meaningful workplace.* Holbrook, MA: Adams Media Corporation.

Trice, H.M., & Beyer, J.M. (1984). Studying organizational cultures through rites and ceremonials. *Academy of Management Review, 9,* 653–659.

van Adelsberg, D., & Trolley, E.A. (1999). Running training like a business. *Training and Development Journal, (53)10,* 56–65.

Walter, K. (1995). Bring on the entertrainment. *Personnel Journal, 74(7),* 84–90.

Chapter 8

FINAL OBSERVATIONS

Lisa A. Burke

Ultimately, training effectiveness (just as organizational effectiveness) is multidimensional, and therefore the steps toward achieving a high-impact training function should not be expected to be ultrasimplistic. This fact no doubt makes a trainer's job more difficult; however, we have attempted to demystify high-impact training strategies and processes in this book by providing straightforward insights and recommendations.

As such, readers should examine relationships among the various topics we've discussed and attempt to maximize the value of their training "products and services" by appropriately affecting change across the training system. This will help trainers to go beyond myopic analyses, one-shot "programs and events," short-term fixes, and incomplete interventions as they begin to consider each of the elements of the training system (for example, needs assessment, program design/development, evaluation of transfer) as necessary, although not sufficient, instruments in the larger web of employee learning and organizational performance. And it will be the companies who embrace this type of approach to employee learning and development that will create and achieve competitive advantage, not merely competitive parity, within their industries.

PUTTING IT ALL TOGETHER: PRACTICAL IMPLICATIONS

As mentioned in the introduction, all of the chapters in this book were generated from many of trainers' top voiced concerns. These issues are ultimately related, as often referenced throughout the book. Even though some connections among topics were directly noted, we should take a closer look at the relationships among all of the chapters—strategic training, needs assessment, training technologies, training transfer, holistic training approaches, and trainer roles—along with their implications. Although in no way totally representative of each author's information and suggestions, this section makes an attempt to outline several integrative themes.

One of the common elements throughout the text is a *strategic* focus—going beyond the all-consuming operational context. A strategic training focus sets the stage for doing so many things right in any training operation. If trainers tie training interventions to the organization's goals, then they will find the needs assessment process much less frustrating. It suddenly becomes much more evident to trainers which performance problems merit a training solution and which require investment, if the group maintains a pivotal role in achieving organizational objectives. The numerous requests from managers for developing more training "programs" as a response to various performance issues is easier to respond to in that it is much more evident to the trainer that not all of these "would-be programs" could be significant contributors to where the organization is going in the long run.

Moreover, a strategic training focus likely increases training transfer in that line managers will begin to see the link between the programs to which they send their employees and their unit's mission. Particularly, in those firms that utilize some form of management by objectives (that is, MBO), where cascading goals in the firm are all interrelated, strategically oriented training helps each unit's managers to support employees in getting their specific area headed in the right direction, in support of minor or major organizational changes.

Furthermore, business-oriented training organizations are more inclined to measure behavioral change from training interventions to ensure success because they see the connection between the two. So, if enhanced customer service is how an organization is going to succeed, and a firm's training focuses on customer service attitudes and behaviors, then the firm is more likely to measure employees on their customer service performance and how they have improved, due to training and other human resource interventions. And training-induced performance changes are probably going to be tracked in the firm's performance appraisal system.

Training technologies that help to manage, support, and instruct employee learning and on-the-job performance are also more apt to be adopted in organizations that link training to their business needs. These technologies can in turn increase outcomes that the training function is most concerned with, such as learning, knowledge and skill enhancement, and job performance improvement. Investments in training technologies will no doubt be facilitated by the support of management, which is most expediently won and maintained by having training "products and services" sell themselves.

One of the other integrative take-aways from this text is that trainers who assume a role of improving employee and organizational *performance*, in any way that they can, whether it be in the form of a job aid, a new technique to improve peer on-the-job coaching, some formal training program, or just a supportive conversation, will directly serve the needs of employees and supervisors in the thick of organizational work. This may well be the most important (new) hat trainers are wearing, that of "a performance architect" so to speak—an individual who looks to build and shape employee performance. The resulting management support is, in part, a product of the payoff supervisors begin to associate with the training function and its creation of holistic performance interventions. If the product is of high quality, "they will return . . . repeatedly"—whether internal trainees or external clients.

Adopting a strategic and holistic performance perspective nicely creates a foundation for a trainer's goals, by underlining the essence of all actions a trainer should pursue in solving organizational and employee performance issues. Such a long-term and comprehensive approach helps to drive the trainer toward business-related solutions by keeping him/her focused on developing training interventions that really matter to the bottom line. Effective needs assessment processes are encouraged if the focus is on "cutting out the fat" and "concentrating on the meat" of potential solutions to performance-based problems. Training technologies then help to appropriately manage, support, and deliver effective training and learning interventions that the trainer decides to pursue, which can also accelerate training transfer back to the job.

Another theme in the book is the importance of management *commitment* and support. Management support has traditionally been won in organizations by those departments or functions that (a) bring in resources, (b) house necessary expertise, (c) enter areas of high uncertainty, or (d) satisfy strategic needs of the firm. For example, sales forces bring in the money to the organization and, therefore, it is not surprising that salespeople tend to receive incredible budgets and resources for executing their jobs. Information systems personnel also tend to garner management support in the form of high (sometimes almost ridiculously high) salaries, benefits, and one-time inducements due to the vital (and currently scarce) expertise they possess with respect to the firm's informational resources. Research and development departments can also command management support in that they venture into unknown territories to create "products" that will meet the firm's strategic need for new, innovative solutions in the marketplace. All of these functional areas then—sales, information systems, and research and development—have enjoyed substantial support across most firms due to the nature of their role or primary task.

Thus, the question becomes—how do high-impact training functions meet similar organizational needs in order to solicit increased managerial commitment? In short, by pursuing and executing the training system more effectively, the trainer's contribution in the firm will become more visible and tantamount to other organizational functions and managers. High impact trainers experience more success, exposure, influence, respect, and recognition in their organizations because they (a) possess sophisticated expertise in employee learning, performance improvement, and organizational development and (b) satisfy strategic needs of the firm by tying performance-based solutions to business needs.

It is this direct "value-added contribution" that many trainers have been neglecting and that has resulted in their lack of organizational success. In these situations, trainers receive unenviable budgets, minimal staff and resources, and they exert little influence among decision makers. But, as we have presented, a more sophisticated approach to training and employee learning has arrived, and it is time to pull the training function up by the bootstraps and make its potential contribution to organizational success obvious and known.

Ultimately, as examined in this book, the primary issues confronting training professionals can be attacked from a practical, yet still grounded, perspective. We have outlined in each topical area useful action plans, frameworks, series of questions, examples, models, and resources to deal with trainers' top issues, basing our prescriptions in current research, literature, and/or extensive experience. As such, we have tried to demystify high impact training practices by making strategic and process-oriented training improvements a bit more uncomplicated.

To this end, one of the last sections of the book includes a suggested resources section that further identifies practical and relevant trainer resources in the form of Internet sites, articles, and books. As more empirical research is conducted and more in-depth case analyses are published, the training literature will become even more advanced in its ability to extend suggestions and recommendations for training professionals.

FINAL COMMENTS

In conclusion, the training and development field is in an exhilarating period of transition in which it is quickly becoming an integral tool in redefining business performance, stimulating employee growth, and executing business strategy. With the insights gained in this book, it is our sincere hope that trainers across the globe will have gained some additional tools and insights that will help them support the continued expansion and contribution of their organization's performance improvement endeavors.

Suggested Resources

Included in this section is a listing of journal articles, books, and Internet sites that are relevant to the various issues discussed in this book (that is, strategic training, needs assessment, training transfer and evaluation, performance consulting, training technology). Each resource could therefore prove to be a valuable additional asset in any trainer's personal training and development resource collection.

ARTICLES

Anthony, P., & Norton, L.A. (1991). Link HR to corporate strategy. *Personnel Journal, 7(4)*, 75–86.

Baldwin, T.T., & Magjuka, R.J. (1991). Organizational training and signals of importance: Effects of pretraining perceptions on intentions to transfer. *Human Resources Development Quarterly, 2*, 25–36.

Bassi, L.J., Benson, G., & Cheney, S. (1996). The top ten trends. *Training and Development Journal, 50(11)*, 28–42.

Bell, J.D., & Kerr, D.L. (1987). Measuring training results: Key to managerial commitment. *Training and Development Journal, 41(1)*, 70–73.

Berry, J.K. (1990). Linking management development to business strategy. *Training and Development Journal, 44(8)*, 20–22.

Bonner, D. (2000). Enter the chief knowledge officer. *Training and Development Journal, 54(2)*, 36–40.

Butterfield, E.C., & Nelson, G.D. (1989). Theory and practice of teaching for transfer. *Education Technology Resource Development, 37*, 5–38.

Carnevale, A.P., & Schulz, E.R. (1990). Evaluation practices. *Training and Development Journal, 44(7)*, S23–S30.

Cusimano, J.M. (1996). Managers as facilitators. *Training and Development Journal, 50(9)*, 31–33.

Davis, M. (1997). Getting workers back to the basics. *Training and Development Journal, 51(10)*, 14–15.

Filipczak, B. (1997). An Internet of your very own. In D. Zielinksi (Ed.), *Using technology-delivered training* (pp. 127–128). Minneapolis, MN: Lakewood.

Fitzgerald, W. (1992). Training versus development. *Training and Development Journal, 46(5)*, 81–84.

Ford, J.K. (1990). Understanding training transfer: The water remains murky. *Human Resources Development Quarterly, 1*, 225–229.

Ford, J.K., & Wroten, S. (1984). Introducing new methods for conducting training evaluation and for linking training evaluation to program design. *Personnel Psychology, 37*, 651–665.

Gainer, L.J. (1989). Making the competitive connection: Strategic management and training. *Training and Development Journal, 43(9)*, S1–S30.

Galagan, P.A. (1990). A CEO's view of training. *Training and Development Journal, 44(5)*, 40–50.

Garavaglia, P.L. (1993). How to ensure transfer of training. *Training and Development Journal, 47(10)*, 63–68.

Garvin, D.A. (1993). Building a learning organization. *Harvard Business Review, 71*, 78–91.

Kelley, K. (1994, March 28). Motorola: Training for the millennium. *Business Week*, 158–172.

Kramlinger, T. (1998). How to deliver a change message. *Training and Development Journal, 52(4)*, 44–47.

Landau, M.D. (2000). Corporate universities crack open their doors. *The Journal of Business Strategy, 21*, 18–23.

McCauley, C.D., Lombardo, M.M., & Usher, C.J. (1989). Diagnosing management development needs: An instrument based on how managers develop. *Journal of Management, 15*, 389–403.

McIntosh, S.S., Page, S., & Hall, K.B. (1993). Adding value through training. *Training and Development Journal, 47(7)*, 39–44.

McMurrer, D.P., Van Buren, M.E., & Woodwell, W.H., Jr. (2000). Making the commitment. *Training and Development Journal, 54(1)*, 41–48.

Marx, R.D. (1986a). Self-managed skill retention. *Training and Development Journal, 40*, 54–57.

Marx, R.D. (1986b). Improving management development through relapse prevention strategies. *Journal of Management Development, 5*, 27–40.

Newstrom, J.W. (1987). Confronting anomalies in evaluation. *Training and Development Journal, 41(7)*, 56–60.

Newstrom, J.W. (1986). Leveraging management development through the management of transfer. *Journal of Management Development, 5(5)*, 33–45.

Noe, R.A., & Ford, J.K. (1992). Emerging issues and new directions for training research. *Research in Personnel and Human Resources Management, 10*, 345–384.

Parry, S.B. (1997). Ten ways to get management buy-in. *Training and Development Journal, 51(9)*, 21–22.

Plott, C.E. (1996). Preparing for 2020. *Training and Development Journal, 50(11)*, 46–49.

Pollack, C., & Masters, R. (1997, February). Using Internet technologies to enhance training, *Performance Improvement*. pp. 28–31.

Quinn, S.R., & Karp, S. (1986). Developing an objective evaluation tool. *Training and Development Journal, 40(5)*, 90–92.

Raghuram, S., & Arvey, R.D. (1994). Business strategy links with staffing and training practices. *Human Resource Planning, 17*, 55–73.

Rosett, A. (1997). That was a great class, but . . . *Training and Development Journal, 51(7)*, 19–24.

Sevilla, C., & Wells, T.D. (1998). Contracting to ensure training transfer. *Training and Development Journal, 52(6)*, 10–11.

Siebert, K.W., Hall, D.T., & Kram, K.E. (1995). Strengthening the weak link in strategic executive development: Integrating individual development and global business strategy. *Human Resource Management, 34*, 549–567.

Tannenbaum, S.I., & Yukl, G. (1992). Training and development in work organizations. *Annual Review of Psychology, 43*, 399–441.

Torrence, D.R., & Torrence, J.A. (1987). Training in the face of illiteracy. *Training and Development Journal, 41(8)*, 44–49.

Tracey, J.B., Tannenbaum, S.I., & Kavanagh, M.J. (1995). Applying trained skills on the job: The importance of the work environment. *Journal of Applied Psychology, 80*, 239–252.

Van Buren, M.E. (2000). Learning technologies: Can they or can't they? *Training and Development Journal, 54(4)*, 62.

Van Buren, M.E., & King, S.B. (2000). ASTD's annual accounting of worldwide patterns in employer-provided training. *Training and Development Supplement: The 2000 ASTD International Comparisons Report*, S1–S24.

Vander Linde, K., Horney, N., & Koonce, R. (1997). Seven ways to make your training department one of the best. *Training and Development Journal, 51(8)*, 20–28.

Weinstein, M.B. (2000). Thirty-three world-class competencies. *Training and Development Journal, 54(5)*, 20–23.

Wexley, K.N., & Baldwin, T.T. (1986). Posttraining strategies for facilitating positive transfer: An empirical exploration. *Academy of Management Journal, 29*, 503–520.

Zemke, R. (1998, March). How to do a needs assessment when you think you don't have time. *Training*, 38–44.

BOOKS

Bader, G.E., & Bloom, A.E. (1994). *Make your training results last*. Irvine, CA: Richard Chang Associates.

Brinkerhoff, R.O. (1987). *Achieving results from training: How to evaluate human resource development to strengthen programs and increase impact*. San Francisco: Jossey-Bass.

Brinkerhoff, R.O., & Gill, S.J. (1994). *The learning alliance: Systems thinking in human resource development*. San Francisco: Jossey-Bass.

Brookfield, S.D. (1986). *Understanding and facilitating adult learning: A comprehensive analysis of principles and effective practices*. San Francisco: Jossey-Bass.

Craig, R.L. (1996). *The ASTD training and development handbook: A guide to human resource development*. Hightstown, NJ: McGraw-Hill.

Dick, W., & Carey, L. 1990. *The systematic design of instruction*. (3rd ed.) Glenview, IL: Scott Foresman & Company.

Ford, J.K. (Ed.) (1997). *Improving training effectiveness in work organizations*. Mahwah, NJ: Lawrence Erlbaum.

Gagné, R.M., & Briggs, L.J. (1979). *Principles of instructional design*. (2nd ed.) Chicago: Holt, Rinehart, & Winston, Inc.

Gagné, R.M., & Medsker, K.L. (1996). *The conditions of learning*. Fort Worth, TX: Harcourt-Brace.

Goldstein, I.L. (1986). *Training in organizations: Needs assessment, design, and evaluation*. Pacific Grove, CA: Brooks/Cole.

Keller, J.M. (1983). Motivational design of instruction. In C.M. Reigeluth (Ed.), *Instructional design theories and models: An overview of their current status* (pp. 386–483). Hillsdale, NJ: Lawrence Erlbaum Associates.

Mager, B. (1984). *Preparing instructional objectives*. (2nd ed.) Belmont, CA: Lake Publishing.

Mager, B (1988). *Making instruction work*. Belmont, CA: David Lake.

Nadler, L., & Nadler, Z. (1994). *Designing training programs*. (2nd ed.) Houston: Gulf Publishing Company.

Nadler, L., & Nadler, Z. (Eds.). (1990). *The handbook of human resource development*. New York: John Wiley & Sons.

Nilson, C. (2000). *Training & Development Yearbook 2000*. Upper Saddle River, NJ: Prentice Hall Direct.

Nilson, C. (1998). *How to manage training: A guide to design and delivery for high performance*. (2nd ed.) New York: AMACOM.

Parry, S.B. (2000). *Training for results*. Alexandria, VA: American Society for Training and Development.

Revans, R. (1984). *The origin and growth of action learning*. London: Chartwell Bratt.

Robinson, D.G., & Robinson, J. (1998). *Moving from training to performance: A practical guidebook*. San Francisco: ASTD and Berrett-Koehler.

Rosow, J.M., & Zager, R. (1988). *Training: The competitive edge*. San Francisco: Jossey-Bass.

Rothwell, W.J. (1996). *Beyond training and development: State-of-the-art strategies for enhancing human performance*. New York: AMACOM.

Rummler, G.A., & Brache, A.P. (1995). *Improving performance: How to manage the white space on the organization chart*. (2nd ed.) Washington, DC: International Society for Performance Improvement and Jossey-Bass.

Van Tiem, D.M., Mosley, J.L., & Dessinger, J.C. (2000). *Performance technology: A guide to improving people, process, and performance*. Washington, DC: International Society for Performance Improvement.

Vander Linde, K., & Biech, E. (Eds.). (1998). *Building high performance: Tools and techniques for training and learning*. Mansfield, OH: ASTD & PricewaterhouseCoopers.

Wade, P.A. (1994). *Measuring the impact of training*. Irvine, CA: Richard Chang Associates.

Wexley, K., & Latham, G. (1991) *Developing and training human resources in organizations*. (2nd ed.) New York: HarperCollins.

INTERNET SITES

Knowledge Transfer Center
http://www.t2ed.com

HR Website
http://www.hr.com

Training and Development Journal
http://www.astd.org/virtual_community/td_magazine/

Training and Development Listserv and other training resources
http://train.ed.psu.edu/TRDEV-L/

Training and Development Research Site
http://www.mapnp.org/library/trng_dev/trng_dev.htm

Training and Development Community Center
http://www.tcm.com/trdev/

American Society for Training and Development (ASTD)
http://www.astd.org

ASTD Consulting Practice Discussion Board
http://www.astd.org/virtual_community/comm_consulting/

ASTD Managing the Training Function Discussion Board
http://www.astd.org/virtual_community/comm_training_function/

"Training Supersite"
http://www.trainingsupersite.com

Academy of Human Resource Development
http://www.ahrd.org

Instructional Design
http://www.coedu.usf.edu/inst_tech/resources/design.html

International Society for Performance Improvement
http://www.ispi.org

Society for Human Resource Management
http://www.shrm.org

The Human Resource Professional's Gateway to the Internet
http://www.hrprosgateway.com/index2.html

Academy of Management
http://www.aom.pace.edu

Society for Industrial and Organizational Psychology
http://www.siop.org

Association of Educational Technology
http://www.aect.org

Society of Applied Learning Technology
http://www.salt.org

Index

About the Editor and Contributors

EDITOR

Lisa A. Burke is an assistant professor of management at Louisiana State University in Shreveport. Professor Burke conducts research and teaches undergraduate and MBA students in management principles, organization theory and design, training and development, and staffing. She received her bachelor's degree in public sector management from the School of Public and Environmental Affairs and her doctorate in organizational behavior and human resource management, both from Indiana University. Dr. Burke also earned her SPHR (Senior Professional in Human Resources) certification from the Society for Human Resource Management in June 1999. Burke previously worked for a large pharmaceutical company, primarily in the training and development area and has consulted in the area of sexual harassment and training transfer. She has presented numerous papers at academic conferences and published various articles in journals such as *Journal of Applied Psychology*, *Human Resource Management*, *Human Resource Development Quarterly*, *The Academy of Management Executive*, *Training and Development*, and *Human Resource Management Review*. Dr. Burke is also on the editorial board for the *Academy of Management Journal*, with research interests including management training, management education, and management development. Professor Burke has received several research awards, including the Innovative Research Design Award and Best Paper

Award from the Management Education and Development Division of the
National Academy of Management.

CONTRIBUTORS

Jennifer W. Guidry has more than fifteen years of experience helping people learn in the workplace. Currently the president of her own training consulting firm, she has designed and delivered custom training for a variety
of Fortune 500 companies in a number of industries. Guidry holds a bachelor's degree in English, with honors, from Trinity College in Hartford, Connecticut, and a master's degree in journalism, with honors, from the
Columbia University Graduate School of Journalism. She is a certified facilitator for Achieve Global, Development Dimensions International (DDI),
and the Blanchard Solutions Group, and an active member of the American
Society for Training and Development.

Larry A. Pace is a management consultant and has actively consulted in
training and development. Pace has provided consultation in the areas of
organizational development, workforce flexibility, skill-based compensation, leadership, and change management. He has also designed and conducted training needs analyses, developed and delivered team-building
interventions, as well as leadership and supervisory training courses. Formerly, Pace was a professor of management at Louisiana State University in
Shreveport and has also taught at the University of Tennessee, Cornell University, and Rensselaer Polytechnic Institute. He has three degrees from the
University of Georgia, including a doctorate in industrial psychology and
psychological measurement. Pace was also a corporate manager (in a Fortune 500 firm) of organizational effectiveness and directed the design, development, delivery, and evaluation of training and consulting programs
in support of employee involvement, total quality, and product delivery
processes.

Janice L. Simmons has over ten years of experience in human resource
and organization development, specializing in human performance and
change implementation. Simmons has worked as an external consultant on
large-scale organizational change projects and as the manager of an internal performance consulting group. Currently, she heads up the leadership
development efforts for a global Fortune 500 company. Simmons holds a
Ph.D. in instructional systems technology from Indiana University.

Joseph V. Wilson III recently retired from a twenty-three-year multifaceted career with a large bank (top 100 nationally), where he was a senior executive vice president. Mr. Wilson's responsibilities included human
resources, corporate development, marketing, affiliate banking, retail
banking, and strategic planning. He also has held senior leadership positions in asset/liability management, property, MIS, data processing, operations, mergers and acquisitions, and auditing. Formerly, Mr. Wilson was a

senior accountant and staff auditor for an international auditing firm. Currently, he is an adjunct instructor and teaches courses in strategy and business policy. Wilson has an MBA with a human resources management concentration from the University of New Orleans, a bachelor's degree in accounting from the University of Mississippi, and has completed graduate-level courses at the New Orleans Baptist Theological Seminary. He is a certified public accountant and has served as a director for several banks and other financial services firms. In addition to his teaching responsibilities, Joey extends his professional experience through personal consulting and motivational speaking.

L. Michael Wykes is a performance analyst and consultant who applies regularly the principles of Human Performance Technology (HPT) to help internal business clients improve performance related to business goals. He has been a successful manager, director, instructor, and instructional designer and has held leadership positions both in education (as a community education director) and in business (as a manager of sales training and as the leader of a corporate leadership development program). Wykes holds two master's degrees, one in human resource development and one in educational leadership. He is a member of the International Society for Performance Improvement (ISPI)—where he has served as a local chapter president—and of the American Society for Training and Development (ASTD). Wykes regularly presents at conferences such as ISPI and ASTD and has presented, by special invitation, to such groups as the New York State Trainer's Association. Wykes' publications include chapter contributions to *Moving from Training to Performance: A Practical Guidebook* (1998) and *In Action: Performance Consulting* (2000). He has also authored a book review for *Human Resource Development Quarterly* and was a prepublication reviewer for *Running Training Like a Business: Delivering Unmistakable Value* (1999, as referenced in chapter 6).